FORUM WIRTSCHAFT 4

Boris-Rolf Dieter

Contract Management in
the German IT-Consulting
Industry

m press >>

Die vorliegende Arbeit wurde 2005 von der Fachhochschule Ludwigshafen als MBA-Dissertation angenommen.

Die Deutsche Bibliothek verzeichnet diese Publikation in der Deutschen Nationalbibliografie; detaillierte bibliografische Daten sind im Internet über http://dnb.ddb.de abrufbar.

m-press ist ein Imprint der Martin Meidenbauer Verlagsbuchhandlung

ISBN 3-89975-535-9

Verlagsverzeichnis schickt gern:
Martin Meidenbauer Verlagsbuchhandlung
Erhardtstr. 8
D-80469 München

www.m-verlag.net

I. Subject

This publication is based on a MBA-dissertation of the postgraduate off-the-job MBA-program in International Management Consulting (MBA-IMC©) of the University of Applied Sciences Ludwigshafen/Rhine, Institute for International Management Consulting (www.i-imc.de). The dissertation was submitted in February 2005 and was rated 1,0 "with distinction".

The original title of the dissertation was "Implementation and Optimisation of a Contract Management Function in the German IT-Consulting Industry: An Exploration to which Extent a Company in the IT-Consulting Industry Can Benefit from a Contract Management Function". Dissertation Supervisor and proof reader was Karl Adolf Scholz, Lecturer at the University of Applied Sciences Ludwigshafen/Rhine, Institute for International Management Consulting, and former managing director of KPMG Consulting / BearingPoint (Deutschland) GmbH, Frankfurt/Main. Second proof reader was Prof. Dr. Christel Niedereichholz CMC, University of Applied Sciences Ludwigshafen/Rhine, Institute for International Management Consulting.

This publication contains the content of the above mentioned dissertation plus the apart from the dissertation published appraisal of the Contract Management expert survey 2004.

"The heart of managing a business is managing its processes."

Michael Hammer[1]

---

[1] U.S. author and academic, in "Beyond Re-engineering" (1996)

II. Abstract

The business relevance of the efficiency of supporting functions in companies has grown steadily throughout the last decade. Parallel to this a new supporting function developed in many industries and companies - the (Sales) Contract Management – without finding much consideration in research and science.

This publication aims to close this gap and to give internal and external consultants, the affected management, their team members and as well as other interested groups well researched background knowledge about the optimisation and implementation of a Contract Management function focussed in the dissertation project on the German IT-Consulting industry.

By providing the reader with detailed descriptions and definitions of the function, various best practices, literature and information hints, representations of procedures and tools he should be enabled to make the decision whether or not his company could benefit from implementing a Contract Management function or optimising their Contract Management function.

In addition this research contains a brief history of the development of Contract Management functions, descriptions of commonly established benefits and problem areas of Contract Management functions and provides detailed suggestions for the analysis, optimisation and implementation of a Contract Management function which are fast and easily transferable into practice. It might serve as well, either autonomously or with external advice, as a base of an actual implementation or an optimisation project of such a function.

Extensive references to other sources of knowledge about Contract Management, a for this special subject first bibliography and a complementary industry survey completes this compilatory work.

The reader will receive the following key information:

➢ **How can Contract Management be defined and delimited?**
➢ **What are the internal and external dimensions of a Contract Management function?**

- ➢ **What are the common benefits of a Contract Management function for a company?**
- ➢ **How can the financial contributions of a Contract Management function be calculated?**
- ➢ **What are the typical problem areas of Contract Management functions?**
- ➢ **How can a Contract Management function be effectively organised or optimised and embedded in the company structure or value chain?**
- ➢ **Which tools and procedures support this objective?**
- ➢ **Which examples of best practices for the optimisation and implementation of a Contract Management function exist in literature?**

The work was carried out from June to December 2004 by desk and field research. In the initial data collection phase literature research was performed and consultations with professional associations, academics of the Contract Management surrounding and Contract Management practitioners were conducted. In a complementary data collection a survey with experts from the academic surrounding of Contract Management and subject matter experts from the major companies (TOP 25 of the "Lünendonk-Liste") of the industry in concern (IT-Consulting) in Germany as a structured random sample were conducted by a questionnaire.

This publication shows that optimisation and implementation activities concerning CM functions open up a huge potential for an increase of administrative efficiency of CM activities. It offers the respective company a significant additional contribution to its financial success and an increase in service quality towards the company´s customers. To realise these benefits through optimisation and implementation activities the research results provide a substantial help.

Although the research field of this publication is limited on Germany, Sales Contract Management and the IT-Consulting industry, it is presumed that the outcome of the publication can be easily transferable to CM functions in other countries, strategic alignments or industries.

III. Table of Contents

9

IV. List of Abbreviations

BA	Berufsakademie (Academy of Applied Sciences)
BITKOM	Bundesverband Informationswirtschaft, Telekommunikation und neue Medien (German Association for Information Technology, Telecommunications and New Media)
BDU	Bundesverband Deutscher Unternehmensberater (Federal Association of German Management Consultants)
CEO	Chief Executive Officer
CFO	Chief Financial Officer
CIO	Chief Information Officer
CM	Contract Management
Dipl. jur. (Univ.)	Diplomjurist - Universität - (graduated lawyer with university diploma)
Dr.	Doktor (philosophiae doctor, PhD)
DGRI	Deutsche Gesellschaft für Recht und Informatik (German Federation for Law and Information Science)
FH	Fachhochschule (University of Applied Sciences)
IBM	International Business Machines Corporation
IACCM	International Association of Contract and Commercial Managers
IT	Information Technology
LL.M.	Magister legum (master of laws)
MBA	Master of Business Administration
p.a.	per annum (per year)
Prof.	Professor (professor)
RA	Rechtsanwalt (attorney-at-law)
ROI	Return on investment
TQM	Total Quality Management
Univ.	Universität (University)

V. List of Figures

VI. List of Tables

VII. Introduction

1. General introduction

Each operative or administrative function in a company influences (more or less) directly the profit a company intends to make with its business activities. Not only the successful activities of an operative function, like the sales department, but also the supporting or infrastructural activities of such a function, like the project office or the Human Resources department, can lead to a significant competitive advantage for the company and can deliver an important contribution to the company´s success[2].

The closer an administrative function is positioned towards the company´s customers and/or the deeper this function is linked with the primary activities of the value chain of the company, the more important and direct can be its impact on the profit of the company[3].

An administrative function that is commonly situated close to the company´s customers and that is, through its close interlock with the sales forces, normally deeply linked with the primary activities of the value chain of the company is the Contract Management function (subsequently abbreviated as CM).

This function is well known in the Anglo-American region and developed in companies with high risk, high value deals where sales success depends upon extensive negotiations (e.g. defence, electronics, heavy engineering and aerospace). Since approximately 10 years this function finds its way to other regions and industries as with the German IT-Consulting industry which is dealt with in this publication[4].

As shown in the following figure in the first phase of the evolution of the sales CM function the sales function traditionally acts as the sole client interface and holds responsibility for the CM activities. With growing need for negotiation in a second phase these responsibilities are handed over frequently to the Legal department. In a third phase commercial professionals begin to emerge within local business units. In the last phase

---

[2] Porter, p. 33+34
[3] Porter, p. 43+44
[4] Garrett, preface, p. VII

a consolidation of the function as a separate CM function and its independence from the Legal department might develop.

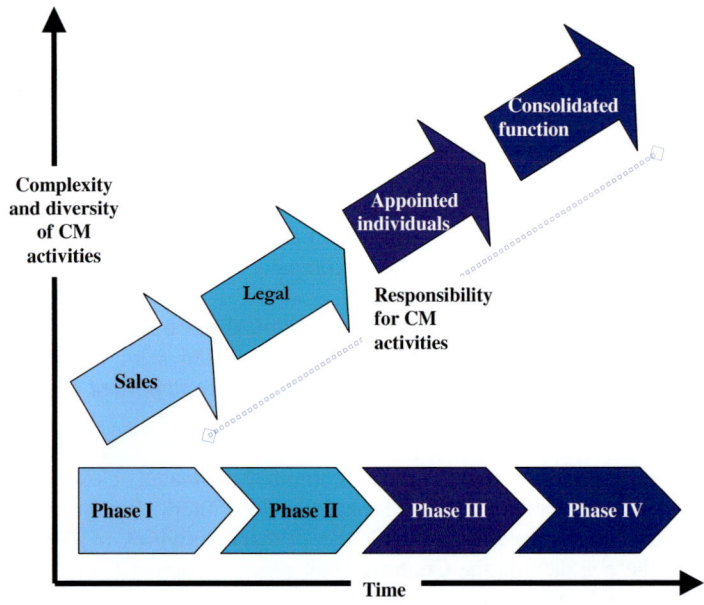

Figure 1 "Evolution of the sales contracting role"[5]

After years of an impressive world wide yearly double digit market growth in the last 30 years the IT-Consulting industry has experienced since 2001, not only in Germany but on a global scale, a tremendous decrease in the overall market volume[6][7].

Due to this rapid market development in the "golden years" of the so called "New Economy", which this industry was an important part of, the strategic focus was merely on growth and not on profit. For this reason

---

[5] IACCM "The Commercial Function: Evolution and Background", p. 1+2

[6] figures and facts for Germany can be found in the Lünendonk list "Lünendonk Liste II 2004", Lünendonk GmbH, 2004

(www.luenendonk.de/html/marktanalysen_listen_it_systemintegration.html), also in parts in the annex of this work

[7] or in the BDU study "Facts & Figures zum Beratermarkt 2002" (Facts & Figures for the Consulting Market 2002), BDU 2003

(www.bdu.de/downloads/UB/Pub/Brosch/Facts_und_Figures_2002.pdf)

14

only little necessity existed to optimise administrative (as well as operative) functions while an increase of profit easily came out of the rising sales volume and not necessarily from operational or functional excellence.

However, in the light of the recession of the last few years this has changed completely. The new economically difficult surrounding forced companies in this industry to increasingly optimise their administrative (and operative) functions to regain or keep up their profitability[8][9].

A significant contribution to this process can add a CM function in general, an implementation/introduction or optimisation through service improvements, increase of efficiency and effectiveness or (intelligent) cost reductions[10][11].

In addition, the relevance of contracts is changing: their role shifts from a purely legal necessity into tools for optimising business relationships. Their complexity, interdependence, number and diversity increases and there is a growing need for managing financial and operational risk that resides in contracts[12]. Moreover it should not be forgotten that contracts may represent in the supply of IT services the only tangible deliverable towards the customer[13][14].

This publication is therefore designed to give the interested reader an overview of the topic. Starting from this CM will be defined and delimited as a function and its dimensions will be explained. From this base optimisation potential and implementation hints are determined and costs and benefits are discussed.

2. Methodology

In order to achieve the stated objectives, desk and field research were performed. The dissertation followed thereby the inductive approach for a (compilatory) research.

---

[8] Kubr, p. 597
[9] Maister, p. 38
[10] IACCM "Contract Management – An Opportunity Still Being Missed?", p. 7
[11] Garrett, preface, VII
[12] PricewaterhouseCoopers LLP "Contract management: control value and minimise risks", p. 2
[13] IACCM learning unit chapter 3 "Overview of Major Types of Relationship", p. 1
[14] Garrett, preface, VII

a) Initial data collection

In a first step there was an intensive search for relevant literature. Relevant literature is written materials that are directly related to the dissertation topic or related to the general topic of the dissertation.

Literature related directly to the dissertation topic

An extensive internet research[15] and a research in the online catalogue of different German university libraries by key words and title words like "Contract Management", "Vertragsmanagement" (Contract Management in German) and "Vertragswesen" (Contract Administration/Management function in German) could not retrieve literature that is directly linked to the dissertation topic. Neither in Germany nor in the Anglophone region literature dealing with "Contract Management in the (German) IT-Consulting Industry" could be obtained. This was confirmed in discussions with some professors and senior practitioners of the authors´ personal CM network.

Literature related to Contract Management

Some literature and training offers which deal in general with CM were found and concerning the literature are listed in the bibliography[16]. In general very little research work has been done concerning the specifics of CM functions. This publication might provide a contribution to close this gap and give an overview of the state of discussion about this topic.

Literature related to general aspects of the organisation or optimisation of administrative functions

Links to the general aspects of the dissertation topic were found in the literature concerning commercial organisation theory. There is a wide range of according publications but as mentioned above nothing specific pertaining CM. General reading[17] had to be transcribed for use in the dissertation.

****

---

[15] at www.google.de and .com, www.buch.de, www.amazon.de and amazon.com
[16] e.g. Heussen, Garrett
[17] e.g. Bühner

B. R. Dieter - "Contract Management in the German IT-Consulting Industry"

In summary the previous materials named in these sections were on the one hand a good starting point for the dissertation. On the other hand it also shows that further ground needed to be explored.

b) Consultations with supervisor and professional organisations

In a second step the topic, aim(s) and objectives of the dissertation were co-ordinated with the supervisor. The structure, methodology and content of the dissertation were subjected to a review by the supervisor.

Contacts to relevant national and international professional organisations[18][19] were installed and consultations concerning sources of information (literature and subject matter experts) were led with them and some subject matter experts.

Synchronised there was a general research for subject matter experts. They were necessary for the expert survey and the quality assurance of the dissertation. For the expert survey a questionnaire form and a cover letter were designed and tested.

c) Complementary data collection

In this step the expert survey[20] was carried out. The number of participants was limited to approximately 20-25. This number seamed from a methodological point of view to be adequate because it can be assumed from experience that the marked out research field can be sufficiently documented with this quantity of interviews. Referred to a well defined research question for data collection empirical a number of 10 interviews with subject matter experts are sufficient. All additional interviews with subject matter experts do not furnish further details concerning the research question but help to cross check the outcome of the first serial of interviews[21].

---

[18] IACCM (www.iaccm.com)
[19] BITKOM (www.bitkom.org)
[20] Dieter, Appraisal of the Contract Management Survey 2004
[21] Niedereichholz II, p. 39

17

The methodological character of the inquiry is defined below:

➢ Structured qualitative survey with a defined suite of direct and predominantly closed questions in a questionnaire and the possibility to add free comments (the questionnaire forms can be found in the annex of this work)

➢ The inquiry was performed as an intersected inquiry (structured random sample) appropriate to the concentration principles of information collection; therefore the so-called "Lünendonk-Liste"[22] was used

➢ The survey was run mostly with external experts, some interviews were run with experts deriving from other business units of the authors own corporate group (IBM) if their company was listed itself in the "Lünendonk-Liste"

➢ One fifth of the questionnaires were filled out by (CM) experts belonging to an academic surrounding (university professors and senior lecturers) or professional organisations (BITKOM and IACCM), four fifths of the questionnaires were answered by CM practitioners from different companies in the IT-Consulting industry; only practitioners from the major companies in the selected industry that are ranked in the TOP 25 of the above mentioned "Lünendonk-Liste" covering the German IT-Consulting industry were admitted

Parallel to the survey an additional literature research was conducted. This literature research was merely motivated from the results from the consultations with the supervisor and the output of the expert surveys.

d) Analysis of data, discussion, conclusion and compilation of dissertation

In this step the collected data was analysed. The consolidated and well structured data was then discussed. Conclusions were drawn and the dissertation was compiled.

---

[22] http://www.luenendonk.de/html/marktanalysen_listen_it_systemintegration.html (also in parts in the annex of this work)

VIII. Definitions and Delimitations

1. Definition of Contract Management (CM)

a) Meaning of the term CM in this publication

In the sense of this publication CM is (if not explicit stated differently):

➢ A primary administrative function (not primarily an operative function)
➢ Occupied with sales contracts (not procurement or employment contracts)
➢ Primarily supporting the sales forces and the senior management (not the customers or other administrative functions)
➢ Covering with its activities the whole lifecycle of a contract (not only the administration of a completed contract)
➢ A function with skill in legal, technical and financial matters pertaining the contracts of the given industry (not only contractual skill)

CM is not:

➢ The (classical) Legal department
➢ A simple and passive contract administration/archive function

Garrett describes analogously thereto CM as

> "...the art and science of managing a contractual agreement throughout the contracting process"[23].

b) Other divergent meanings of the term CM

In some publications the term CM is used in the sense of "contracted management", "management by contracts" or "contractor management".

The sense of CM as "contracted management" is used when the managing director of a company is not employee of the company but in his position by a contract with another organisation (e.g. as part of a

---

[23] Garrett, p. 1

19

development aid project or installed by the corporate group of the company).

The sense of CM as "management by contracts" is used when a company performs the main activities in a certain service unit itself but has to co-ordinate through this unit accessory activities by several contractual interfaces to suppliers.

The sense of CM as "contractor management" is used for the activities that are necessary to manage and co-ordinate suppliers or subcontractors.

These divergent meanings of CM do not apply to this publication.

2. German IT-Consulting industry

The focus in this work is on CM functions for sales contracts in the German IT-Consulting industry. This industry includes companies that are creating more than 60% of their turnover with IT-Consulting, development of individual software or systems integration.

This definition follows the subdivision the market leader for market analysis in the German consulting industry, the Lünendonk GmbH, utilises in their research[24].

3. General delimitations

The publication will not treat the following adjacent aspects of CM functions:

➢ Legal aspects of CM, contract design or contract execution
➢ The negotiation process[25]
➢ Remuneration questions in CM functions
➢ Motivation elements or incentive systems for CM staff
➢ General problems of re-structuring, implementation / introduction or optimisation projects
➢ General aspects of creating functional strategies for CM functions[26]

---

[24] http://www.luenendonk.de/html/marktanalysen_listen_it_systemintegration.html html (also in the annex of this work)
[25] interesting reading provides Garrett, p. 129-142 or Ury, p. 1 ff.
[26] for this topic the major market research companies provide various reports: e.g. www.aberdeen.com, www.gartner.com, www.metagroup.com and www.gs.com

- A market research on available CM software tools[27]
- Outsourcing of CM functions
- (Contract) risk management

---

[27] a source of information about this topic can be the study of AMR Research from February 2003 with the title "The Compelling ROI of Contract Management" (available over www.amrresearch.com) or the study of the University for Technical Science and Architecture in Freiburg (CH) from April 2003 with the title "Contract and Risk Management Software" (available over www.symfact.ch)

IX. Organisational Dimensions of CM Functions

The decision whether or not to implement and/or to optimise a CM function is only possible and can only be successful if there is a deep familiarity with the organisational dimensions of such a function. The description of these dimensions is subject of the following chapters.

In general CM can be described in two different sorts of organisational dimensions: external and internal dimensions. The external dimensions are descriptions of representations that define the outer connection of a CM function to their surrounding. The internal dimensions are descriptions of representations that characterise the interior organisation and set-up of a CM function.

1. External dimensions

The external dimensions of CM function are the following:

a) Intra-company interfaces

CM has relevant interfaces to the following internal functions that have to deal with and/or determine sales contracts. It is presumed for this work that these functions are not part of an outsourced company unit.

The listed tasks behind the denotation of the function are examples for conjoint responsibilities or demarcation areas.

- **Sales department:** e.g. determination of contract portfolio, negotiation authority
- **Procurement/Supply Chain Network:** e.g. co-ordination of subcontractor purchase, co-operation contracts policy
- **Legal department:** e.g. special law cases, legal proceedings
- **Patent office:** e.g. patent applications, patent infringement
- **Accounting:** e.g. accrued liabilities for debatable contracts, check of creditworthiness
- **Controlling:** e.g. pricing policy, elaboration of calculation sheets
- **Project administration:** e.g. interpretation of contract clauses, invoicing problems
- **Project management:** e.g. contract execution rules, contract modification guidelines

- **Operational management team:** e.g. signature authorisation, latitude of contractual acting
- **Senior management team:** e.g. predefinition of general standard terms and conditions, contract quality and review policy
- **(Technical) quality assurance function:** e.g. quality and feasibility audits, (technical) risk evaluation, approval authority
- **Human resources department:** e.g. labour law cases, obtaining work permits

It should not be forgotten that CM is not only tied closely to different functions in a company but is also embedded in certain processes of a company.

For example, in the product development process, CM must be an important part as CM has to secure that new products are covered by adequate terms and conditions that reflect the specifics of the product and the interests of the target markets[28].

b) Extra-company interfaces

CM has relevant interfaces to the following external functions:

- **Legal practises** (instead of a own Legal department or in addition to it): e.g. representation in legal proceedings, provisioning of specialised legal skill
- **Administrative authorities**: e.g. applying for administrative licences
- **Customers**: e.g. their Legal department, their CM function, their procurement department or single Project, Commercial or Contract Managers

The character of these interfaces can be that the CM function is in the role of a supplier or in the role of a customer.

---

[28] IACCM CM learning unit chapter 1 "How Contractual Relationships Are Formed & Why They Matter", p. 4+5

c) Strategic alignment

The strategic alignment of a CM function should derivate from the company´s strategy and should aim to support the desired effects of the CM function.

The two dimensions to define the strategic alignment are:

➤ **Customer contact** (merely direct or indirect)
➤ **Focus of the CM activities** (primary on risk minimisation or maximisation of turn-over)

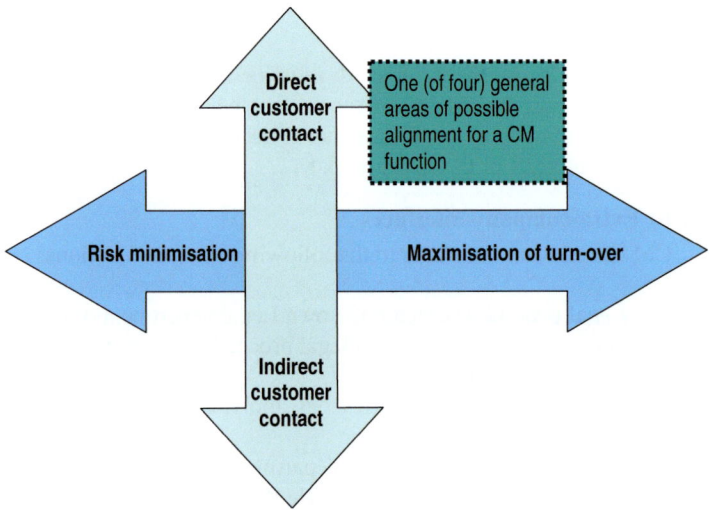

Figure 2 "Dimensions of strategic alignment"

Having direct customer contact means that the CM function has the authority to develop an own communication with the customer or being the only point of contact with the customer in contractual matters. Having indirect contact with the customer means that the CM function has no customer contact and acts only as a back office in contractual matters for e.g. the sales forces.

Having a focus on the maximisation of turn-over means that the primary goal of the CM activities is to help the sales forces and the operative management to increase revenue. In this case the CM function will be seldom found in conflict with the sales function or the operative management because a parallelism of objectives exist. Having a focus on the minimisation of risk means that the primary goal of the CM activities is to prevent, discover and manage risks. In this case the CM function has to face frequent conflicts with the sales function and the operative management because their objectives, the short term orientated and risk friendly sales objective of increasing profit or revenue and the long term orientated and risk unfriendly CM objective of minimising risks, differ (at first sight) cardinally.

Between the four combinations of the two dimensions of strategic alignment a CM function has to be collated (as in the example in the figure above: a CM function with direct customer contact and a primary focus on maximisation of turn-over). This does not exclude that the other representations are without importance for the activities of the CM function. They are not in the foreground of the activities of the CM function and figure a secondary role. The equilibrated combination of risk minimisation and maximisation of turn-over can for example form an own strategic target: profit maximisation. Another possibility to develop a strategic alignment sets the internal differentiation of the CM team; one part of the team can be orientated on direct customer contact and the combination target "profit maximisation", the other part of the CM team has no customer contact and focuses primary on risk minimisation.

A reason to promote a direct customer contact of the CM function can be, for example, to profit from the leverage of the negotiation skill of CM, the volume and complexity of a contract or to provide the customer with a professional correspondent in contractual matters. A reason to prevent direct customer contact of the CM function can be based on tactical aspects or the maturity of the CM function.

A matter of which primary focus (risk minimisation or maximisation of turn-over) is given to a CM function can be for example the risk surrounding of the company´s business, the competitive background of the company´s industry or magisterial constraints.

In most cases an alignment between the both extremes of the two above mentioned dimensions will offer the company the greatest benefit. When the most reasonable proportion is to be equilibrated long experience and comprehensive knowledge are requested in two areas: the CM surrounding and the company´s business model.

A survey[29] with CM experts in the German IT-consulting industry in the course of the dissertation furnished the following figures for the ideal representation of the above mentioned strategic alignments:

Focus:	
primary focus on <u>risk minimisation</u>	**81%**
primary focus on <u>maximisation of turnover</u>	**19%**
and	
Customer contact:	
predominantly <u>direct</u> customer contact (e.g. negotiation lead)	**60%**
predominantly <u>indirect</u> customer contact (e.g. sales back office)	**40%**

Table 1 "Strategic alignment preferences of German CM experts"

Others contiguous aspects of the strategic alignment are treated in other chapters (e.g. resource allocation, reporting line, hierarchical integration, service attitude) and should be kept in mind while developing the strategic alignment of a CM function.

d) Resource allocation

Resources can be allocated in two dimensions. One dimension is the **local allocation**; the other dimension is the **thematic allocation**. These allocations are as well applicable to a CM function.

Local allocation for a CM function means either to install CM as a centralised function (in one location), as a remote function (in several locations) or as a mixture between these representations.

Thematic allocation for a CM function means to deploy CM either parallel to the organisation of the company´s operative area (e.g. due to topical aspects as customers, technology, industries, solutions, services, functional sectors, projects or geographical aspects like locations, plants, countries, regions, continents), detached from that, as a mixture of both extremes or even without a thematic allocation.

---

[29] Dieter, Appraisal of the Contract Management Survey 2004, question 1

A survey[30] with CM experts in the German IT-consulting industry in the course of the dissertation furnished the following figures for the ideal representation of the above mentioned resource allocation:

Local allocation:	
centralised (e.g. in the company´s headquarters)	30%
decentralised (e.g. in several locations)	17%
merged function	52%
and	
Thematic allocation:	
according to geographical aspects (e.g. regions)	17%
according to topical aspects (e.g. products)	26%
multidimensional (e.g. according to projects and certain contracts)	48%
no thematic allocation	9%

Table 2 "Resource allocation preferences of German CM experts"

To assist the definition of the resource allocation a matrix eventually combined with a communication analysis[31] may be helpful. Such a matrix (some examples are inserted) could have the following layout:

---

[30] Dieter, Appraisal of the Contract Management Survey 2004, question 2
[31] Niedereichholz II, p. 171-174

Local allocation / Thematic allocation	centralised function	remote function	merged function
geographical aspects	e.g. CM function in the company´s headquarters is assigned to regions	e.g. CM function in each plant is assigned to sales territories	e.g. the CM function with central full-time and local part-time Contract Managers is assigned to continents
topical aspects	e.g. CM function in the company´s headquarters is assigned to industries	e.g. CM function in each plant is assigned to certain projects	e.g. the CM function with central and local full-time Contract Managers is assigned to technologies
multi-dimensional	e.g. CM function in the company´s headquarters is assigned to services, key accounts and countries	e.g. CM function in each plant is assigned to countries, certain contracts and solutions	e.g. the CM function with central and local full-time Contract Managers is assigned to functional sectors, major customers and plants
without thematic allocation	e.g. CM function in the company´s headquarters works universal-thematic	e.g. CM function in each plant works universal-thematic	e.g. the CM function with central and local full-time Contract Managers works universal-thematic

Figure 3 "Resource allocation matrix"

Guiding for a decision concerning the local resource allocation should be, for example, the extent of local support that is necessary (or wished), the essential range of co-operation with other central or regional functions or the useful degree of direct collaboration between the individual CM employees.

Decisive importance for the thematic resource allocation should have, for example, the necessity of a tight linkage between CM and the operative area of the company (following the key account, industry, product/solution portfolio or sales organisation structure), language regions, the required client adjacency or the complexity or difficulty of the topic that is handled by the affected business unit.

e) Hierarchical integration

A CM function can be hierarchically integrated in different ways. How it is done depends on the management system[32] a company has implemented. The main integration types are listed below:

➢ **Own department** (in the operative or administrative area of a company)
➢ **Subdivision of a main department** (in the operative or administrative area of a company)
➢ **No own department** (individuals incorporated in the operative or administrative area of a company)

These main types follow the two dimensions in which their modifications can be grouped:

➢ **Hierarchical independence** (organised in an own department, sub-department or in no own department) and
➢ **Organisational integration** (organised as an administrative or as an operative function)

Hierarchical independence influences the degree a function is dedicated by itself, has a transparent task profile for their (internal) clients and forms its own proper sphere of professional development. In the case of CM this is suggestive for the delimitation of a CM function to the sales department or, even more significant, to the Legal department. For this delimitation a strengthening of the role profile of CM can be useful and can give a CM function an autonomous profile that does not lead to the

---

[32] Wöhe, p. 152-158

assessment of CM as a "minor Legal department" or "subordinate sales function".

Organisational integration influences the character of a function as cost (administrative function) or profit (operative function) centre. In the case of CM this organisational integration can be destining for the focus of the CM activities (see to this chapter "strategic alignment").

To support the definition of the hierarchical integration a matrix can be beneficial. Such a matrix (some examples are inserted) could have the following layout:

Organisational integration / Hierarchical independence	administrative function	operative function
own department	e.g. CM department in the company´s headquarters	e.g. the CM department has strong linkage to the sales force with shared profit and loss responsibility
sub-division of main department	e.g. the CM function is a sub-division of the Legal department	e.g. CM is sub-division of the sales department
no own department, incorporation in other departments	e.g. the responsible CM personnel is integrated in different departments of the company´s headquarters (project office, controlling etc.)	e.g. the responsible CM personnel is fully integrated in the business units

Figure 4 "Hierarchical integration options"

In which way a CM function should be hierarchically integrated in a company is primarily determined by the company´s vision, mission and (functional) strategy. Aspects as they are mentioned in other chapters of this work (e.g. service attitude, strategic alignment, resource allocation) should as well guide this decision.

A survey[33] with CM experts in the German IT-consulting industry in the course of the dissertation furnished the following figures for the ideal representation of the above mentioned hierarchical integration:

Organisational integration:	
as administrative function (e.g. as a cost centre)	78%
as operative function (e.g. as a profit centre)	22%
and	
Hierarchical independence:	
CM forms an own department	39%
CM is sub-division of an (other) department (e.g. Legal, controlling, Procurement, quality assurance or project team/management)	48%
CM staff is incorporated in other departments	13%

Table 3 "Hierarchical integration preferences of German CM experts"

f) Reporting line

There are different reporting lines possible for a CM function. Which one is selected depends upon the strategic role or independence that is favoured for the CM function. For example, a benchmarking survey[34] about sales CM activities indicates, on a world-wide and cross-industry level, the following significance:

Reporting line to:	Percentage of allocation types:
Legal	20%
CEO	20%
Finance	18,46%
Business Units	16,92%
Operations	13,85%
Others	8,16%
CIO	1,54%

Table 4 „Reporting lines"

Similar aspects as they are mentioned in other chapters of this work (e.g. service attitude, strategic alignment, resource allocation,

---

[33] Dieter, Appraisal of the Contract Management Survey 2004, question 4
[34] IACCM "Corporate Benchmarking Study", Question 1.2.

hierarchical integration) are also strongly related to this decision and should be observed.

A survey[35] with CM experts in the German IT-consulting industry in the course of the dissertation furnished the following figures for the recommended reporting line:

Reporting line to:	
Manager of the Legal department	16%
CEO	45%
CFO	3%
Manager of the or a business unit	29%
Operations manager	3%
CIO	3%
Others	0%

Table 5 "Reporting line preferences of German CM experts"

2. Internal dimensions

The internal dimensions of a CM function are the following:

a) Tasks and disciplines

The tasks and disciplines in CM can be generally grouped in five to six phases[36] [37] [38]. These phases form the CM process. The phases are named and exemplified with specific activities below.

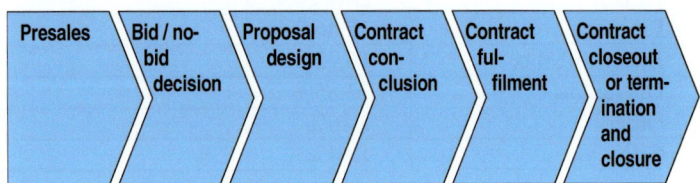

Figure 5 "Phases of the CM process"

---

[35] Dieter, Appraisal of the Contract Management Survey 2004, question 3
[36] Garrett, p. 3-5
[37] Tybussek, p. 4 ff.
[38] Heusen "Vertragsmanagement und Vertragsgestaltung", p. 18

All the listed tasks and disciplines can (but must not) belong to the responsibilities of a CM function. If they are performed in a company and through a CM function is a question of strategy, corporate structure and culture, project and contract management capabilities of a company[39].

These tasks and disciplines also form the job description of a Contract Manager. Examples for (internal) job descriptions for Contract Managers in a certain company can be found in a lot of companies or can be educed from job advertisements.

When analysing the activities a CM function performs a functioning ("what is done?"), a collaboration ("in which role – responsible/assisting/information addressee - is it done?") and a communication ("which and in which extent communication flows?") analysis[40] can give important hints for optimisation potential and problem areas.

The list should show a set of activities that is usually performed by a CM functions and that should be kept in mind while implementing or optimising a CM function. The phases are described in the following order:

1. **Presales phase**
2. **Bid/no-bid decision phase**
3. **Proposal design phase**
4. **Contract conclusion phase**
5. **Contract fulfilment phase**
6. **Contract closeout or termination and contract closure phase**

<u>**during the presales phase**</u>[41]

> Proactive research for changes and new tendencies in the legal environment and their preparation for intra-company use
> Training of other CM personnel, sales staff and operative management

---

[39] Garrett, p. 19
[40] Niedereichholz II, p.171-177
[41] examples for best practices in the sellers preaward phase gives Garrett, p. 83+84

33

- Maintenance of process documentation, contract standards and supporting documents or tools (e.g. integrating in user feedback and optimisation hints, updating legal instructions)
- Developing new contract forms and/or terms and conditions
- Provisioning of additional documents for proposal design (e.g. official verifications, balance sheets and profit and loss accounts, staffing figures)
- Counselling for other units of the company
- Involvement in business or product development
- Involvement in competitive research, market analysis and benchmarking
- Definition of handling schemes for (contractual) crisis scenarios
- Definition of early warning systems for contractual problems

during the bid/no-bid decision phase

- Support in collecting and understanding of customer and other (legal, magisterial and self-evident) requirements
- Supporting collection of past experience with the customer (e.g. former winning and/or loosing proposals)
- Support of formal risk assessment ("identify – analyse – mitigate")
- Support of formal opportunity assessment
- Consultation in bidding decision making process

during the proposal design phase

- Support of the formation of the proposal team
- Drafting statement of work or service level agreement
- Reviewing statement of work or service level agreement
- Consultation in proposal design
- Ensuring risk minimisation and quality assurance for the proposal (proposal check -> concerning contract clauses: comprehensive check; concerning risk analysis, calculation and technical description of the solution: validity check)
- Supporting or steering technical and financial approval process

during the contract conclusion phase

- Negotiations or tactical negotiation support
- Primary contract reviews
- Support of the proposal team

34

➤ Support of the formal communication between customer and own company

during the contract fulfilment phase[42]

➤ Briefing of the delivery team concerning contractual obligations
➤ Communicating the contract content to all affected functions
➤ Contract administration
➤ Support of contract execution
➤ Support of contractual change management and its documentation
➤ Manage contract/relationship
➤ Contract controlling (e.g. monitoring compliance with the contract terms and conditions)
➤ Contract interpretation
➤ Support of service level or deliverables management
➤ Support of supplier controlling
➤ Consultation in contract problems (e.g. support in resolving claims and disputes)
➤ Secondary contract reviews
➤ Ensuring risk minimisation and quality assurance for the signed contracts
➤ Legal project management[43 44 45] (e.g. managing the legal requirements and contractual problems in a project)
➤ If necessary contract annulment and rewinding-up

during contract closeout or termination and after contract closure

➤ Completion of documentation of CM activities
➤ Collecting data for measurements
➤ Evaluating customer satisfaction
➤ Help to fulfil legal and administrative retention requirements concerning storage of records
➤ Lessons learned procedures ("collect – analyse – communicate")
➤ Process improvements
➤ Supporting project or process audits

---

[42] examples for best practices in the sellers postaward phase gives Garrett, p. 174-176
[43] Kulartz, p. 69-71
[44] Bartsch, VIII No. 2
[45] Kapellmann, p. 1 ff.

A survey[46] with CM experts in the German IT-consulting industry in the course of the dissertation furnished the following figures for the recommended coverage of CM phases and the significance of CM support in these phases for the company´s success:

Phases coverage:	
1. presales	39%
2. bid / no-bid decision	52%
3. proposal design	74%
4. contract conclusion	74%
5. contract fulfilment	61%
6. contract closeout or termination and closure	78%

Table 6 "CM phases coverage preferences of German CM experts"

Significance of CM support (1 = low; 10 = high):		
1. for presales	average	3,4
2. for the bid / no-bid decision	average	4,8
3. for proposal design	average	7,4
4. for contract conclusion	average	7,3
5. for contract fulfilment	average	5,0
6. for contract closeout or termination and closure	average	5,9

Table 7 "Estimation of significance of CM support per CM phase of German CM experts"

In addition to that a benchmarking survey[47] about sales CM activities indicates, on a world-wide and cross-industry level, the following significance:

---

[46] Dieter, Appraisal of the Contract Management Survey 2004, question 5
[47] IACCM „Corporate Benchmarking Survey", Question 1.1.

CM activity	Is this activity part of the CM responsibility? (percentage of "yes" answers)	How much CM resources are consumed by this activity? (average)
pre-bid support / vendor selection	0%	0%
bid support / management	40,2%	18,1%
develop contracts / terms & conditions	60,8%	24,8%
negotiation	50,3%	23,8%
manage contract / relationship	41,3%	18,4%
general contracts / commercial advice to other parts of business	48,3%	15,2%
Develop / manage contract standards / process / practices / tools	55,2%	12%

Table 8 „CM activities and allocated resources"

In all the above mentioned phases a documentation of the performed tasks and disciplines is necessary. The documentation should be extended to any major steps in the performed activities.

Minimum prerequisites of tasks, disciplines and documentation for an DIN/ISO certification can be found in the DIN/ISO norm catalogue[48]. The applicable norm catalogue for the given industry is (DIN EN) ISO 9001:2000. In the chapters 5.2, 7.2.1-3 of this norm catalogue the minimum prerequisites of CM activities are described.

Information about what a certification or quality program in the consulting industry means can be obtained in literature[49][50].

---

[48] www.din.de/www.iso.ch (not gratuitously obtainable)
[49] Kubr, p. 597-613
[50] Maister, p. 79-95

b) Qualification and skills

As an interdisciplinary function performing CM tasks implies a broad knowledge in different areas. This knowledge is not linked to a dedicated qualification or skill but to a certain set of qualifications and skills.

Legal skill is surely one of the most important qualifications for a Contract Manager but also other qualifications and skills are essential to perform CM tasks.

For a Legal department Heussen[51] gives the following numbers for the consumed resources of certain activities of such a department. Deriving from these numbers for a CM function the percentage of exclusively legal activities (legal review, assessment and realisation) can then be supposed as a little bit smaller than the below mentioned numbers:

Activity:	Percentage of consumed resources:
Fact finding	30%
Internal communication and decision	20%
External communication and organisation	20%
Legal review, assessment and realisation	30%

Table 9 "Activities of a Legal department and percentage of consumed resources"

Necessary qualifications for a CM function are (alternatively):

➢ Legal education (not necessarily a graduation in law)
➢ General business administration or business engineering education (not necessarily a graduation in business administration or business engineering)

Necessary skills for a CM function are (accumulative):

➢ Technical understanding
➢ Industry experience or knowledge
➢ Project management skills

---

[51] Heussen "Rechtliches Risikomanagement", p. 13

38

- Negotiation know-how
- Communication and social competence
- Language skills (e.g. legal and business English)
- Training competence
- Process understanding

While rarely one single person can fulfil all the above listed requirements to their full extent a well-balanced skill mix in the CM team is of great importance. Interdisciplinary skill building and frequent skill transfer in the team should be encouraged. Very specialised skill or high-level skill that is rarely used should be bought in (by outsourcing or suppliers). Low-level tasks should be covered by paralegal, team assistants, trainees or graduands.

To raise and control the team qualification formal internal maturity assessments, external certification/licensing[52] [53] and/or skill bench-marking should regularly be used.

As primary sources of further professional information, skill development and subject area knowledge are the adequate means: external training, conferences, formal "lessons learned" process, learning on the job, internet, law firms, surveys, focus groups, competitive research, new employee interviews, mentoring and internal classes.

Trainings that are dealing in a wider or closer sense with CM are offered by several major training providers like "Euroforum"[54], "Forum-Institut"[55], Management Circle[56], "University of Washington – UW Extension"[57] and "ESI International"[58].

---

[52] e.g. IACCM offers a certification program to individuals or at the corporate level (information at www.iaccm.com)
[53] Kubr, p. 130-132
[54] www.euroforum.com ("Der Contract Manager/The Contract Manager")
[55] www.forum-institut.de ("Organisation der Rechtsabteilung/Organisation of the Legal Department" oder "Das strategische Profitcenter Rechtsabteilung/The Strategic Profit Center Legal Department")
[56] www.managementcircle.de (Vertragsmanagement für Nichtjuristen/Contract Management for Non-Lawyers")
[57] www.outreach.washington.edu/ext/certificates/com/com_crs.asp ("Certificate Program in Contract Management")
[58] www.esi-intl.com ("Vertragsverhandlung und –gestaltung für Projektmanager/Contract Negotiations and Design for Project Managers")

A target of the team development should be to reach a lucid and distinguished skill profile. This enables the internal client to find, un-delayed, a problem solution partner and helps them to align the CM function on their special tasks and disciplines.

A survey[59] with CM experts in the German IT-consulting industry in the course of the dissertation furnished the following figures for the recommended qualification and skills:

Qualification:	
Apprenticeship (commercial, technical or with focus on quality assurance; but only as additional qualification to a study)	18%
Study	100%
Course of study:	
Academy of Applied Sciences (BA)	18%
University of Applied Sciences (FH)	38%
University (Univ.)	38%

Table 10 "Preferred qualification for CM profession"

Field of study:	
Law (Univ.)	29%
Economic law (FH)	29%
Business administration	24%
Business engineering	18%
Named others : information/computer science, business information science, engineering or double qualifications like LL.M. plus MBA or national equivalent	

Table 11 "Preferred field of study for CM profession"

---

[59] Dieter, Appraisal of the Contract Management Survey 2004, question 6

Skills:	
Technical understanding	78%
Industry knowledge and experience	83%
Project management skills	70%
Negotiation know-how	83%
Substantial communication and social competence	87%
Language knowledge (e.g. legal English)	57%
Experience as trainer	9%
(CM-) process understanding	83%
Named other skills: ability to cope with stress, national/international mobility, legal competence (contract law), know-how in quality management, quality assurance and risk assessment, experience in risk management, technical IT knowledge, experiences with proposals and contracts as well as with problem cases of the industries´ contracting practice	

Table 12 "Necessary skills for CM profession"

c) Forms of contracts or proposals

The form of contracts and proposals used in a company are significant parameters for the adequate skill level and organisation structure of a CM function. Together with the volume of usage of the different forms of contracts or proposals (e.g. grouped in an A-B-C-classification) they can give hints for the optimisation or implementation potential of a CM function.

Usually different forms of contracts or proposals are used in the CM business. Which of them are handled by the CM function and which of them belong to the standard contract portfolio of the company depends on the company´s contracting policy. This policy is linked with the common content of the contracts in the company´s industry, the applied consulting products, the complexity or risk level of the projects, the runtime of the engagements, the proposal or contract requirements (e.g. in the public sector) and the commitments that were given to the client in the acquisitions phase. The volume of contracts or proposals can therefore range from only oral consent to thousands of pages[60].

---

[60] Garrett, p. 9

Another aspect influencing the form of a contract or proposal are the contracting methods used in the company´s industry. They differ from competitive to non-competitive and simplified to formal methods.

Contracting approach	Competitive	Non-competitive
Simplified	- purchase cards - imprest funds or petty cash - auctioning	- purchase agreements
Formal	- sealed bidding - two-step sealed bidding - competitive proposals - competitive negotiations	- sole-source negotiation - single-source negotiation

Table 13 "Contracting approaches"[61]

Frequent forms of contracts or proposals are:

➢ **Oral contract:** no written documentation of the mutual agreed contract contents exists (only advisable for short and simple engagements, succession orders or in cases of total trust and well versed in professional practice; should the occasion arise revenue recognition problematically)

➢ **Think piece:** a very short (e.g. one page) version of a proposal or contract when no request for proposal exists

➢ **Confirmation letter:** a very short (e.g. one page) version of a proposal or contract issued by the consulting company when the customer has decided to work with the consulting company

➢ **Letter of agreement** (or of engagement, of appointment, of confirmation): a short version of a proposal or contract issued by the customer and referring to a certain proposal when he has decided to work with the consulting company

➢ **Letter proposal:** a short (e.g. two pages) version of a proposal or contract when a request for proposal exists

➢ **Draft proposal:** a version of a proposal or contract that is still under discussion

➢ **Final proposal:** a version of a proposal or contract that is thought of as the base of the contract with the customer

---

[61] Garrett, p. 51-59

> **Customer specific proposal:** a version of a proposal or contract that is edited with customer specific forms and contents (e.g. often the case in the public sector)
> **Unsolicited proposal:** a version of a proposal or contract when no request for proposal or former customer contacts exists

Further details and examples for these types of contracts or proposals[62] [63] or their pricing arrangements[64] can be obtained in literature.

Documents named LOI (letter of intend) and MOU (memorandum of understanding) are normally no proposals or contracts. They are only pre-contract agreements that establish the intention of the parties to buy or respectively sell services or products in future[65].

Master (or purchase, universal sales, distributor, supply framework or basic ordering) agreements are not listed above as they are not dedicated for a single engagement but for an indeterminate number of engagements or transactions. Master agreements serve as (customised) general conditions for particular proposals and contracts as do the general terms and conditions[66]. They are used by over 90% of all (sales) CM functions[67] and cover a considerable part (approximately 50-80% of all transactions in one third of the participating companies) of all contractual transactions[68].

The main types of technical contents of the above mentioned contracts or proposals can be grouped in products, services, solutions, outsourcing / managed services, channels / alliances and licensing[69]. General information about specific contractual proposal or contract contents can be obtained either through competitive research or in literature[70] [71].

The layout of a contract or proposal should not just be seen as a technical or legal document but also as a marketing instrument. The contract or proposal must therefore be prepared (preferably by the consulting

---

[62] Niedereichholz I, p. 205 ff.
[63] Kubr, p. 163-165
[64] Garrett, p. 85-113
[65] Garrett, p. 113
[66] Garrett, p. 112
[67] IACCM „Master Agreement Survey", Question 3
[68] IACCM „Master Agreement Survey", Question 4
[69] IACCM „Corporate Benchmarking Survey", Question 1.3.
[70] Niedereicholz I, p. 201 ff.
[71] Kubr, p. 160-164 and Appendix 5

company and not by the customer because of the often underestimated power of the "editing sovereignty"[72]) in a professional manner that covers marketing, technical and contractual needs[73].

d) Authority to decide

A CM function has through its interdisciplinary character and its multiplex tasks and disciplines multifaceted tangential points with the sphere of responsibility of other administrative and operative functions in the company. This requires a clear definition of the respective authority to decide[74].

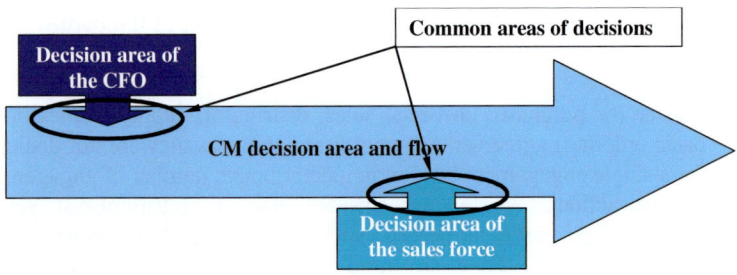

Figure 6 "Decision areas"

Such a definition can start with the description of the general (vertical) CM decision area and the (horizontal) CM decision flow. Both will have overlaps with neighbouring functions. In these common areas of decisions the role and responsibility of CM and the neighbouring functions has to be defined and documented (e.g. in an approval guideline) in a transparent way.

Of the perspective of CM and the internal clients this documentation must fulfil the sequential requirements:

> **What can be decided by CM** (concerning topic and/or extent; e.g. only standard situations or also case by case exceptions)?
> **What can be only partly decided by CM** (e.g. due to powers reserved of the Legal department or the CFO)?

---

[72] Garrett, p. 138
[73] Garrett, p. 79
[74] Garrett, p. 18-20

> **Which role has CM in the decision** (e.g. binding end approval or non-committal statement after review[75], single point of exchange of formal communication with the customer[76])?
> **What is not permitted to be decided by CM?**
> **Who is then in charge for the decision?**

Examples for overlaps for instance with the Legal department are the overall contract ownership or the definition of the overall contract strategy. Overlaps with the sales department exist in the setting of the overall negotiation strategy, the evaluation of cost and the setting of cost or price.

Another area of overlap with the legal and sales department is the negotiation authority concerning the different parts of the contract. For example a benchmarking survey[77] about sales CM activities indicates, on a world-wide and cross-industry level, the following figures:

Negotiation authority of CM:	Percentage of consent:
All terms	40,63%
Most terms	35,94%
Legal terms only	4,69%
Business terms only	6,25%
No negotiation authority	12,5%

Table 14 „Negotiation authority of CM"

e) Internal structure

In the design of the internal structure of a CM function certain aspects are important. These aspects are:

> A reasonable mixture of junior and senior CM staff (e.g. 50%:50%)
> Installation of a backup concept (every skill, task, important contract or client should be occupied by a minimum of two colleagues, one as primary point of contact and one as backup)
> Clear internal scopes and responsibilities
> Definition of clear competence and decision profiles
> Transparent archiving rules

---

[75] Garrett, p. 138
[76] Garrett, p. 152
[77] IACCM „Corporate Benchmarking Survey", Question 1.7.

45

> Lucid internal hierarchy (e.g. between the CM team leader, the CM team co-ordinators and the CM staff members; between central and regional CM representatives)

The observance of these aspects supports the acceptance of a CM function by the customers, the management of the company and other internal functions.

f) Size

The size of a CM function and if it can be exercised in part-time or full-time employment is strongly related to the tasks and disciplines such a function has to perform and the profundity of their execution. An extensive standardisation of contracts (e.g. selling mostly based on fixed standard terms and conditions) or a high degree of business transaction through uniform contractual bounded resellers can massively reduce CM sumptuary and hence the needed size of a CM function. Other aspects that influence the ideal size of a CM function can be: the complexity and range of the handled contracts, the legal character of the contracts, the business/sales model, the maturity of the sales force in contractual matters, the extent of preparations of the proposal by the proposal writers, the grade of difficulties within the customer relation, the scope of the contract, the quality and quantity of the projects or technical, commercial and legal conditions that are defined by the customer.

A survey[78] with CM experts in the German IT-consulting industry in the course of the dissertation furnished the following figures for the capability of possible parameters for the size of CM functions:

---

[78] Dieter, Appraisal of the Contract Management Survey 2004, question 7

46

Parameters:	
Turnover per (experienced; full time regular) CM employee	9%
Number of proposal writer, contract owner etc. per (experienced; full time regular) CM employee	26%
Ratio of turnover to budget of the CM function	0%
Number of contracts per (experienced; full time regular) CM employee	65%
Other named parameters: number of standard contracts that has to be modified, number of customer dates, quantity of escalations in the course of a project number of externally defined (by customers or suppliers) contracts	

Table 15 "Capability of parameters for the size of a CM function"

Another parameter can be the span of control that is necessary to reach sustainable influence on the contracting quality. To attain a reasonable span of control in the CM competence area it should be tended to that all non-standard contracts and 10-20% by number and 30-40% by overall sales revenue of all standard contracts are submitted to a CM review[79].

As an additional example for the reader, the author cites the benchmarking survey[80] about sales CM activities which indicates, on a world-wide and cross-industry level, the following figures:

Sales people per CM professional:	Percentage of assignment:
Up to 10	13,33%
11-30	10%
31-75	18,33%
76-200	10%
201-500	16,67%
More than 500	31,67%

Table 16 "Sales people per CM professional"

---

[79] diverging figures for sales Contract Management functions on a world-wide and cross-industry level contains the IACCM "Corporate Benchmarking Survey", Question 3.2.
[80] IACCM „Corporate Benchmarking Survey", Question 3.3.

g) Service level

To measure their own efficiency and to manage (internal) client relationship and satisfaction a CM function should define a clear service level agreement. Such an agreement for a CM function should cover the designated aspects as follows:

- **Clear priority rules** (e.g. which tasks are the most important tasks, which tasks are only secondary, what job sequence has to be abided by)
- **Service times** (e.g. in which period of time CM stands by, does emergency numbers exist for non-service times)
- **Reaction intervals** (e.g. in which time limit a CM answer in a certain request can be expected)
- **Service in general** (e.g. which services provides CM)
- **Process definitions** (e.g. descriptions of all CM processes and adjacent documents)
- **Interfaces descriptions** (e.g. definitions of all interfaces and points of contact to other internal or external functions)
- **Processing rules** (e.g. which tasks are processed in which way and with which intensity)
- **Quality guidelines** (e.g. which quality must have the output of the CM activities)
- **Consistent task profile** (the internal clients should know what the tasks of CM are and to whom they have to address certain questions or jobs; the number of forwarded jobs should thus be minimised to speed up the problem solution)
- **Communication rules** (e.g. how and when communication should be done)
- **Internal empowerment guidelines** (e.g. how and in which cases can CM tasks or authorities be delegated to other functions or individuals)
- **Contact matrix** (e.g. who is in charge for the contact to a certain business unit, customer or other internal or external function)
- **Delimitations to other functions** (see also the chapter about "authority to decide" and "intra-company interfaces")
- If applicable: **cost of CM consulting or service charges**

To give the supported function a reasonable service the above mentioned aspects of a service level should fulfil the following demands[81]:

---

[81] Heussen "Rechtliches Risikomanagement", p. 12

➤ **Fast:** solutions for standard problems must be provided immediately
➤ **Engaged:** CM must be actively involved in the contracting process and not act as a distanced and passive function that has to be involved by others but not by itself
➤ **Reliable:** in non standard problems a quick access to specialist knowledge must be available

h) Service attitude

To perform a successful CM operation the CM team should have a distinct service mentality. Target of the CM activities should be to support their internal clients as professional, business oriented and applicatory as possible.

It should be clear for the team members that the CM responsibilities have a direct impact on the company´s customer relationship because the proposal is the first work sample towards the client, because contracting behaviour also form the brand image, because contracts and proposals are precedents for the customer for future business[82] and because that contracts are an important asset for doing business or creating a competitive advantage.

The CM staff should be convinced by a holistic view of contracting as an important driver for improved business performance by aligning terms with market needs, enabling information flow, improving governance and risk management and be able to communicate this to their internal clients.

To facilitate such a service mentality designated rules should be adhered to:

➤ **CM activities should be performed proactively rather than reactively** (e.g. the CM activities should aim to foresee problems and prevent them and not to start activities when the problem has already occurred)
➤ **CM should be committed to completed staff work** (e.g. it should be aspired to handle one case by one person in full extent without partly relegating it to other functions to minimise communication efforts and cycle times for the internal client)

---

[82] Garrett, p. 176-177

- **CM focus should be on quick response, short answering times, speed of decision making and execution support** (while as a rule the dynamic of acting is different in the operative area than in the legal or administrative area, CM has to reach for a balance of the different celerity e.g. a common inquiry must be answered without delay on the whole by the contacted CM employee and is only when very special know-how is needed routed in parts to other function or colleagues for further processing)
- **Output of CM activities should focus on creating revenue or cost reduction** (e.g. the CM function should regularly evaluate its activities if they lead to a financial contribution to the company´s success or if they lead to a reduction of costs)
- **In the CM function an understanding must be in place that high quality in contracts means high profitability in business** (and this should permanently be communicated to the proposal writers)
- **Knowledge management must have a high priority for CM** (e.g. solutions for problems or a first bypass should be stored in a common database for reuse to speed up the problem solving process)
- **CM aims to provide comprehensible support** (e.g. CM answers are orientated upon the knowledge of the requester, they "translate" legal language into business language or "condense" highly complex problem constellations to pragmatic operational instructions or suggestions)
- **CM drafts understandable contracts and with easily recognisable options** (e.g. contract language and contract layout is orientated upon the users´ needs and comprehension horizon)
- **CM has a high provision of effective support for internal clients** (e.g. the CM function can be regularly evaluated by an internal survey of the demands of their internal clients concerning the CM support and from this new service offers can be concluded)
- **CM covers contractually the complete service portfolio of the company** (e.g. for all standard contracting situations CM can provide a prototype proposal or contract)

Depending on the company´s strategy the attitudes of CM functions often shifts through guidelines as above in the following way[83]:

From:	To:
Cost and risk focus	Strategic contributor and competence
Control and monitoring	Driving innovation (our own and our suppliers)
Bottleneck in time to market	Committed partner in product introduction
Reactive to change, requirements	Proactive modification of process, practice and terms
Image as inhibitors, bureaucrats	Enablers, partners in executing superior deals and relationships

Table 17 "Former and future mission of CM"

i) Support tools

The efficiency of the CM activities can be significantly raised by support tools. Relevant support tools are:

➢ **Workflow software systems** (e.g. to image and automate a complex contract approval process or the contract creation)
➢ **Contract management software** (e.g. to administrate commitment management, risk tracking and change management)
➢ **Internal databases** (e.g. for contract clauses, variations of clauses, general information, guidelines and reusable assets)
➢ **Contract repository** (e.g. to store all contracts electronically, to allow access to terms and clauses within contracts and to combine this data with analysis capabilities)
➢ **External database access**
➢ **Internet**
➢ **CD-ROM**
➢ **A CM Library**
➢ **Competitive research** (e.g. new employee interviews, surveys, focus groups, contacts to professional organisations and major law firms)
➢ **Highly standardised contract templates, general terms and conditions and support documents**

---

[83] IACCM "Contracting as a Strategic Competence", p. 7

51

j) Workplace equipment

To practise the CM activities in an adequate way the standard workplace equipment should comprise of a PC with internet access, a telephone and the customary office services.

To enhance productivity access to a general secretary and assistance services is advisable.

To foster mobile working a laptop and a mobile phone should replace or supplement the PC and the normal non-mobile telephone.

k) Measurements

To determine the success (e.g. risk containment, motivation of good risk decisions within the contracting process) and the ongoing optimisation of CM activities, measurements must be in place. These measurements must derivate from the vision and (functional) strategy of the company and transform them into operative tasks for the CM function. If the measurements are not in line with these goals no substantial support of the company´s strategy can be expected.

To support and to operationalise the strategy of the company a balanced scorecard can be designed for CM. As the four topics for the CM balanced scorecard perspectives as "processes", "innovation/skill", "(internal) clients" and "(financial) contribution" are conceivable. These four perspectives must then be detailed with targets, ratios, defaults and measurements[84].

Parameters for the balanced scorecard or key indicators for CM functions could be e.g. (internal) client satisfaction, skill level benchmarks or improvements, salary benchmarks, process cycle or lead times, skill level, percentage of contracts under the company´s own standard terms and conditions, revenue improvements, savings/cost reductions, costs of contract negotiations and management compliance with CM standards or reaction times.

---

[84] Wöhe, p. 218

X. Benefits of a CM Function

This chapter is a collection of different sources of information of which benefits a well functioning CM function can provide a company.

In addition an example for a rough "ROI" calculation model of the financial benefit of CM activities is sketched to show the measurable financial contribution a CM function can effectuate.

1. Descriptions of benefits

The international professional association of Contract and Commercial Managers (IACCM) detected in inquiries the following business benefits by improved CM activities[85]:

- **Improved business control** (e.g. improved and more consistent negotiation strategies, improved customer loyalty, better assessment and management of risks, better and more informed management review and decision making)
- **Greater replication of solutions** (e.g. greater adoption and use of world wide standards, simplified contract production and higher quality of contracting)
- **Reduced cycle times** (e.g. faster review and approval processes, proactive term management)
- **Improved efficiency and accuracy** (e.g. reduction in errors, reduction in disputes, improved change management and greater revenue from changes, increased revenue from renewals)
- **Significant gains in corporate image** (e.g. through greater responsiveness and higher level of accuracy)

PricewaterhouseCoopers[86] names in an independent paper the following impacts deriving from an effective CM:

- **Understand and control risk** (e.g. meeting regulatory requirements and mitigating the impact of low-profitability)
- **Realise huge cost savings** (e.g. through arising opportunities in the course of manually renewing and realigning contracts)

---

[85] IACCM "Contract Management – An Opportunity Still Being Missed?", p. 3
[86] PricewaterhouseCoopers LLP, p. 17

> **Uncover opportunities to enhance revenue** (e.g. through relieving sales employees from time-consuming administrative duties related to contracts)
> **Gain administrative efficiency** (e.g. taking away routine tasks from skilled staff)
> **Improve customer service** (e.g. through faster creation of customer contracts and more efficient handling of queries)

Nextance[87], a CM software provider, found the following possible impacts of an automated and well functioning CM function:

> **Increasing revenue** (through negotiating better contracts, invoicing for all services rendered, collecting penalties and charges and up-sell or cross-sell opportunities)
> **Decreasing cost** (through avoiding overpayments, leveraging global pricing and discount opportunities, cutting unnecessary contract renewals, reducing hidden costs or penalties and reducing audit costs)
> **Reducing risks** (through preventing risk, mitigating risk and ensuring regulatory compliance)
> **Maximise productivity through process excellence** (through finding duplicate contracts quickly, simplify and streamline operations and contracts compliance, improve visibility, share information and consistent business processes)

An additional listing of (financial) benefits of a CM function named by German CM experts can be found in the appraisal of the survey that accompanied the dissertation[88].

To reach these benefits through an optimisation or implementation project requires in most cases the consolidation of different problems areas. These are described in the chapter after next.

2. Calculation model: financial benefit of CM

To verify the necessity and the financial contribution of a CM function a rough "ROI" calculation should be carried out. Such a calculation can have for instance the following design and can be configured more detailed if this should be necessary for the users´ needs.

---

[87] Nextance Advisory Services, p. 5-8
[88] Dieter, Appraisal of the Contract Management Survey 2004, question 8

Some examples for exemplification are inserted. The quoted numbers and assumptions are based on the authors own experience figures.

CM activity	Possible effect	Situation / Assumptions	Potential results	Financial impact
Training of proposal writers (e.g. one training day for approximately 15 participants, effected by one Contract Manager, mandatory for everyone who wants to write a proposal or deals with proposals, not only account managers)	Higher proposal quality followed by an increasing win rate (e.g. from 1:10 to 1:7)	For a company to reach holding only 1.000[89] active sales contracts p.a. means (with the given win rate) to write 10.000 proposals p.a.; if the proposal design consumes in average only 1 h the sum of 10.000 h p.a. in total (= approximately 1.250 working days á 8 h) are consumed for proposal design	30% less effort for proposal design means approximately 375 working days p.a. more in disposal for other value creating activities	(375 x 8 x average sales staff cost per hour) – total cost of training days p.a. = financial benefit p.a.
CM activity	Possible effect	Situation / Assumptions	Potential results	Financial impact
Proposal check (presumed is in average only 2 h for each proposal in the CM	Detecting a pricing or sumptuary estimation error in a proposal (e.g. price is 1,5%	For a company that calculates in average with 6% profit this means to reach in this	With 1.000 active contracts p.a. and an estimated occurrence rate of 5% this	(1.000 x 5%) x (average contract volume/price x 1,5%) – cost of proposal

---

[89] the typical Fortune 1000 company maintains approximately 20.000 to 40.000 active contracts at any given time; Aberdeen Group "Contract Optimization: A Recession-Proof Strategy for Maximizing Performance and Minimizing Risks", p. 3

check scope, e.g. all non-standard proposals and all standard proposals with higher volume)	too low)	case a mere fourth of the planned profit	means that in 50 contracts p.a. profit is not according to plan through pricing or sumptuary estimation errors	check (= cost of Contract Manager per hour x 2) = financial benefit p.a.
CM activity	**Possible effect**	**Situation / Assumptions**	**Potential results**	**Financial impact**
Contract repository (e.g. an electronic database with some simple controlling and adminis-tration functionality)	Every contract is easy to find, to evaluate and to provide	It is presumed that every contract of the above mentioned 1.000 active contracts p.a. is needed only once a year and the (successful) search and provision of the contract necessitated without a contract repository 1 h more than with it	1.000 h of unproductive effort less for locating a contract	(1.000 x 1) x average secretary staff cost per hour – cost of contract repository p.a. = financial benefit p.a.
CM activity	**Possible effect**	**Situation / Assumptions**	**Potential results**	**Financial impact**
Pre-customised standard proposals	The time for the individual proposal design is through the pre-customisation	It is presumed that for the above mentioned 10.000 proposal p.a. o,5 h less per	5.000 h p.a. less effort for proposal design	5.000 x average senior consultant cost per hour - cost of pre-customisation

56

	reduced	case is needed for proposal design		= financial benefit p.a.
CM activity	**Possible effect**	**Situation / Assumptions**	**Potential results**	**Financial impact**
Negotiation support	CM leads major negotiations or gives tactical support	It is presumed that of the above mentioned 10.000 proposal p.a. 25% are negotiated and that through the CM support the negotiation time efforts is reduced approximately by one fifth	In 500 cases 20% less effort for negotiations	((10.000 x 25%) x average negotiation effort in hours x 20%) x average manager cost per hour - cost of negotiation support = financial benefit p.a.

More calculation examples can be easily developed from the later in this publication mentioned problem areas of CM functions and the listed best practices for CM implementation or optimisation projects.

XI. Problem Areas of CM

To reach the full extent of the above named benefits it is essential to be familiar with the typical problem areas of CM. With this specific knowledge a CM optimisation or implementation project can be much more effectively planned and the (in many cases hidden) optimisation potential much better and directly assessed than through just analysing the situation in the given company without incorporating the experiences of many other companies in this area.

Through the consideration of this knowledge about typical problem areas of CM in the preliminary study or the analysis phase the goal-directed planning of such a project, the overall success of the project, the task definition and the creation of quick wins can be substantially improved.

Following different sources of information about frequently detected CM problem areas are presented.

A survey of a CM software vendor[90] with over 100 companies of the Global 2000 from all industries participating indicates the following major problem areas in CM:

Problem areas	Problem exists in company
Concerns in finding contracts (in less than one day or at all)	81%
No management of contractual commitments through contract lifetime	75%
Major concerns through contractual risks	75%
No or rare tracking of side letters	66%
Belief that their contracts have language that increases corporate risk	63%
No ideas of the interdependencies among their contracts	61%
No tracking of contingent liabilities	60%
No access to specific terms and clauses without looking through contracts	54%
No knowledge about the expiration dates of all their contracts	52%
No enforcement of terms	52%

---

[90] Krappé, K., Kallayil, G., p. 3

No reliable process to alert the correct function or person to respond to a triggered risk	51%
No analysis of contracts by vendor, customer, product or service line possible	51%
No management of negotiated terms across the enterprise	45%
No reliable milestone notification process	40%
No reliable process to update financial systems in the case a risk event occur	40%
No risk evaluation process before sign-off	34%
Large incremental revenue opportunities misdealt by managing sales contracts badly	31%
No use of standard templates to create new agreements	26%
Dissatisfaction with risk closure in the financial reporting	26%

Table 18 "Problem areas in contract control"

IACCM[91] names the following sources of weakness of CM:

➢ **Failure to ensure adequate mutual understanding of the parties expectations**
➢ **Lack of monitoring / failure to establish metrics that give early warning of potential problems**
➢ **Poorly defined and reactive processes for problem resolution**
➢ **Little or no structured approach to assessing impacts of changing conditions on contracts (market, economic, technical etc.)**
➢ **Poor information flow and knowledge management in relation to contract obligations and experience**

In addition IACCM identified the following inhibitors[92]:

➢ **Lack of executive champion** (e.g. no decisions or fragmented decisions in different parts of the business)
➢ **No clear view of potential ROI**
➢ **Lack of resources to focus on this topic**
➢ **Uncertainty concerning the readiness of CM software products**
➢ **Compatibility and overlap with other systems**

---

[91] IACCM "Contract Management – An Opportunity Still Being Missed?", p. 2
[92] IACCM "Contract Management – An Opportunity Still Being Missed?", p. 3

Aberdeen Group[93] identified in his research the following chief barriers to effective CM:

> **Lack of formalised CM procedures**
> **Inefficient, labour-intensive processes**
> **Limited visibility into corporate contracts**
> **Ineffective monitoring and management of contract compliance**

PricewaterhouseCoopers LLP lists the following risks inherent to bad CM[94]:

> **Contracts lacking critical terms**
> **Loss of contract files or documents**
> **Missing contractual deadlines and commitments**
> **Customer undercharged**
> **Vendors overcharging**
> **Time and productivity inefficiency**
> **Uncontrolled impact of external events and new regulations**
> **Competitive disadvantage**
> **Compromised customer loyalty**
> **Loss of key knowledge when key employee leaves**

Nextance[95] found the following challenges in effectively managing contracts:

> **Deferral to less favourable terms**
> **Difficulty to spot rogue contracts**
> **Lack of visibility into contracts**
> **Inability to ensure compliance in fulfilment phase**
> **Invoices can not be matched to contract**
> **Greater contract risk**
> **Missing capitalisation of opportunities written in the contract**

An additional listing of problem areas of a CM function named by German CM experts can be found in the appraisal of the survey that accompanied the dissertation[96].

---

[93] Aberdeen Group "Contract Optimization: A Recession-Proof Strategy for Maximizing Performance and Minimizing Risks", p. 5-9
[94] PricewaterhouseCoopers LLP "Contract management: control value and minimise risks", p. 5
[95] Nextance Advisory Services, p. 2
[96] Dieter, Appraisal of the Contract Management Survey 2004, question 9

The obvious huge optimisation potential of the above mentioned problem areas should lead to their strict observance in CM optimisation and implementation activities. Their analysis should form an important part in the design of a CM optimisation or implementation project.

XII. Suggestions for the Design of a CM Optimisation and Implementation Project

If a company plans to unleash the leverage of the above mentioned benefits and wants to investigate their specific problem areas a CM optimisation or implementation project has to be installed.

1. Project design

Optimising or implementing a CM function is a normal re-structuring project and follows usually the basic structure of such a (consulting) project[97]:

- **Preliminary study**
- **Assessment of existing situation**
- **Drafting of concept of aimed situation**
- **Definition of the optimisation / implementation tasks**
- **Planning of realisation**
- **Realisation**
- **Project evaluation**

Another approach to install such a project can be to use existing structures as e.g. a TQM system[98].

The specific elements of the above demonstrated basic project structure for the implementation and/or optimisation of a CM function are described below.

2. Situation assessment

Helpful for assessing the existing situation are checklists. Such a checklist can, for example, follow the structure and titles of the chapters above that describe the internal and external dimensions of a CM function. Another structure can be deducted from the above listed problem areas of CM.

---

[97] Niedereichholz I, p. 253
[98] Bausinger, p. 3 ff.

Such an assessment checklist can be designed like this:

Assessment Area	Assessed Situation	Comments
a) Size	- 4 contract manager (100%) - 1 contract manager (75%) - 1 paralegal assistant (80%) - 1 administrative assistant (50%)	- sales revenue 160 Mio. EUR (2003) - approximately 4.500 contracts / proposals a year - 900 sales people - actual CM budget: 500.000 EUR
b) Workplace equipment	- PC with internet access - Telephone - Customary offices services - Access to secretary service and administrative assistance	
c) Other areas......	....	....

Table 19 "Checklist sample for CM assessment"

A helpful catalogue of questions that can be used to evaluate the weak points of a legal risk management system suggests Heussen[99].

Parallel to evaluating the existing situation (if not yet done in a preliminary study) a rough version of a cost-benefit analysis can be compiled.

3. Definition of the aimed situation and setting of tasks

After having assessed the current situation, a design of the aimed situation and the setting of optimisation or implementation tasks can be initiated.

a) Measurement plan

The definition of the aimed situation and the setting of tasks can be supported by a measurement plan. Such a plan can be designed like this:

---

[99] Heussen "Rechtliches Risikomanagement", p. 27+28

Assessment Area	Assessed Situation	Aimed Situation	Task	Date	Responsibility
I) Size	ratio CM staff to sales people 1:149	ratio CM staff to sales people 1:100	employment (first internal than external search) of another 2 contract managers and 1 paralegal assistant	till Q2 2005	H. Dupont
II) Workplace equipment	no mobile working facilities	mobile working should be promoted	equipping each Contract Manager with a mobile phone and a laptop instead of a PC	till 30th of July	M. Smith
III)	.....	......	......	....	....

Table 20 "Measurement plan sample"

This measurement plan can then be used to compile a more detailed cost-benefit analysis to support the decision to continue or to stop the project or to change the project scope.

b) Best practices

In literature some examples of best practices can be found that can help in the definition of tasks for a CM optimisation or implementation project.

As best practices PricewaterhouseCoopers LLP[100] suggests:

1. Assign responsibility for the process of managing contracts
2. Define a process that proactively seeks benefits
3. Establish a central repository of information
4. Use technology to support your process

---

[100] PricewaterhouseCoopers LLP, p. 6

Nextance[101] determined the following best practices for CM:

Create
- Standard templates and libraries
- Workflow and version control for collaborative creation
- Exception-based review and approval

Store
- Central contract repository
- Enterprise-wide anytime, anywhere access
- Search, analysis and reporting capability

Manage
- E-mail notification of dates and milestones
- Integration with other enterprise systems
- Tracking and notification of contractual risk
- Configuring contract processes to business needs

To improve or establish (sales) CM activities Garrett[102] recommends the following best practices:

- **Use a CM methodology**
- **Commit to a CM professional development program**
- **Take advantage of electronic commerce and electronic data interchange**
- **Adopt value-based pricing where sensible**
- **Use universal sales agreements**
- **Conduct risk versus opportunity assessments**
- **Simplify standard contract terms and conditions**
- **Employ highly skilled contract negotiators**
- **Hold pre-performance conferences**
- **Adopt a uniform solicitation, proposal and contract format**
- **Use alternative dispute resolution (ADR) methods to resolve disputes**
- **Develop and maintain a best-practices and lessons-learned database**

---

[101] Nextance Advisory Services, p. 1
[102] Garrett, p. 183-186

As areas in which quick wins can be realised by actions to raise contract control are named[103]:

> **Enable visibility and access**
> **Optimise contract creation**
> **Create an obligation and commitment management**
> **Install a contract risk management**

A model for drafting a CM function that provides a competitive advantage for a company can be found in the publications of the Aberdeen Group[104]. For the "best in class" it is defined as:

Organisation: Contract group formalised on a company wide basis. This group enforces standard contract language and direct parameters of acceptable contract decisions. Contract policies and strategies co-ordinated company wide, with high level of involvement/support of CFO and Global Sales executives. Contracting and audit tightly aligned.

Process: Contracting processes standardised company wide. Formal contract templates established and enforced for all products/services, clauses and terms. Automated contract reviews and authorisation routing integrated into extended sales process and systems. Automated service and billing milestone tracking linked to customer relationship management and auditing systems.

Knowledge: Central contract repository shared company wide. Able to search all contract information. Proactive alerts of contract milestones, billing and payments. Able to search and assess clauses and terms. Ability to execute automated profitability and risk analysis of contracts and individual clauses on demand.

Technology: Contracts created, negotiated and reviewed using web-based contract management system that supports authoring, collaboration, approval routing, monitoring, analysis and reporting capabilities. Single sales contract management systems architecture company wide.

---

[103] Krappé, K., Kallayil, G., p. 7
[104] Aberdeen Group "The Sales Contract Management Competitive Framework", p. 1-5

66

Performance metrics: Compliance and performance measured in real-time. Risk proactively assessed based on performance and market dynamics.

Aberdeen research suggests that the quickest and most effective method for achieving contract optimisation is the use of a Web-based contract management solution that offers the following[105]:

➤ **Automate the complete contract life cycle**
➤ **Ensure a high degree of usability for all stakeholders** (e.g. sales, purchasing, executives, Legal etc.)
➤ **Provide an "active" repository for all contracts**
➤ **Systematically integrate with other business systems**
➤ **Provide tools for analysis of contract performance**

---

[105] Aberdeen Group "Turning Contracts into Competitive Advantage", p. 1-4

XIII. Conclusion

The publication shows that the optimisation and implementation of a CM function opens a huge potential for an increase of administrative efficiency of CM activities and functions and can offer the respective company a significant additional contribution to its financial success.

To realise these benefits and to decrease problem areas through optimisation and implementation activities following the research results certain aspects have to be observed.

First of all a CM function has to be tied closely to different neighbouring internal and external functions. It is especially tied to functions with which CM has conjoint responsibilities or that have to deal with or determine sales contracts, as with the sales department or the Legal department, a close contact and an effective cooperation has to be developed. Besides this CM has to be embedded in processes that directly or indirectly influence the CM activities or working areas (e.g. the product development process or the procurement process).

When organising a CM function this research work shows that a strategic alignment that enables a primary focus of the CM activities on risk minimisation and that gives CM direct contact to the customers in the CM competence areas (e.g. negotiation or contract skill) is seen as the best model. Allocated local as a merged function (with mostly centralised and partly decentralised activities) and a multidimensional thematic allocation seems to be the most favourable option. To promote and secure the above mentioned strategic focus and the hierarchical and decision independence, an organisational integration such as an administrative function, in an own department or sub-division of another department is demanded.

To align CM with the needs and interests of its primary customer, the operational area of the company, it is advisable that, under protection of its thematic independence and authority to decide, CM has either, as mentioned above, an integration in an operational department of the company or that it has a direct reporting line to operational management functions like the CEO or the management of a or the business unit.

This research shows that it is presumed that CM renders the highest benefit by focussing its activities not in the presales or bid decision phase of the

CM process but in the proposal design, contract conclusion, contract closeout and to a minor extent in the contract fulfilment phase.

Concerning the necessary qualification for the CM profession it was proved that a study preferably at a university or university of applied sciences especially in (commercial) law or business administration (or occasionally in business engineering) is needed to perform CM activities comprehensively. Required skills are technical understanding, industry knowledge, project management skills, negotiation know-how, substantial communication and social competence and (CM) process understanding. Training experience is demanded rarely and language knowledge only in an international surrounding.

The result of the investigation of the dissertation for parameters for the ideal size of a CM function was unsuccessful. It could only be established that parameters like the number of contracts per CM employee and to a less degree the number of proposal writers and contract owners or turnover per CM employee can, under consideration of the special conditions of the company´s organisation, the contracting approach, the wanted service level, the demanded service attitude, the used support tools and the business surrounding, help to equilibrate CM resources with the given workload.

XIV. Appendix

A. "Lünendonk-Liste" (Luenendonk list) 2004

Ranking of the TOP 25 IT-Consulting and systems integration companies in 2003 in Germany (only the listing, the detailed explanations are not attached).

	Company	Revenue in Mio. Euro		Employees		
		2003	Domestic revenue	2002	2003	2002
1	IBM Business Consulting Services, Stuttgart *)	920,0	920,0	-	-	-
2	Lufthansa Systems Group GmbH, Kelsterbach *)	610,7	610,7	557,7	4.400	4.200
3	Accenture GmbH, Kronberg *)	585,0	585,0	594,0	3.600	3.606
4	Gedas AG, Berlin	576,0	151,0	619,0	4.751	4.814
5	CSC Ploenzke AG, Wiesbaden	575,0	421,5	608,0	4.911	4.823
6	Capgemini Deutschland Holding GmbH, Stuttgart 1)	437,0	437,0	458,0	3.055	3.124
7	BearingPoint GmbH, Frankfurt am Main *)	420,0	420,0	488,9	2.800	3.277
8	Atos Origin GmbH, Stuttgart 2)	285,0	285,0	250,0	2.400	2.200
9	SAP SI Systems Integration AG, Dresden	280,3	223,4	293,2	1.859	1.744
10	Deutsche Post ITSolutions GmbH, Bonn	232,0	232,0	244,0	1.300	1.211
11	IDS Scheer AG, Saarbrücken	221,2	108,7	181,4	1.639	1.381
12	msg Systems AG, Ismaning	182,0	166,1	162,0	1.650	1.450
13	LogicaCMG Deutschland GmbH & Co. KG, Hamburg	170,9	170,9	211,2	1.922	2.094
14	ESG Elektroniksystem- und Logistik-GmbH, München	160,0	155,5	143,0	1.003	932
15	Itelligence AG, Bielefeld	145,6	72,6	168,5	1.068	1.465
16	Materna GmbH, Dortmund	142,0	127,4	153,0	1.115	1.200
17	IT-Services and Solutions GmbH, Chemnitz	140,0	140,0	143,0	1.300	1.300
18	Softlab GmbH, München	139,0	107,0	164,0	1.100	1.114
19	GFT Technologies AG, St. Georgen	138,1	103,6	155,7	1.043	1.204
20	sd&m Software Design & Management AG, München	119,0	119,0	129,0	877	897
21	Unilog Holding GmbH, Tübingen	100,0	100,0	113,0	786	1.111
22	SerCon Service Consulting GmbH, Böblingen	94,0	94,0	125,0	1.066	1.276
23	Beratungsgruppe Plaut Deutschland, Ismaning	81,2	49,5	216,0	550	1.366
24	Danet GmbH, Weiterstadt	68,4	55,3	90,1	675	740
25	Novasoft AG, Heidelberg	61,4	24,1	72,0	441	474

1) till April 2004 Cap Gemini Ernst & Young GmbH

2) 09/2003: Acquistion of the IT-Consulting division of Schlumberger Sema
*) Data partially estimated
- = no details obtained

Admittance criteria for this list: more than 60% of their turnover is attained with IT-Consulting, development of individual software or systems integration.

N.B.: The rule of precedence for this ranking is based on inspected self information of the companies and estimations of the Lünendonk GmbH about in Germany or from Germany arising balanced/produced revenues. COPYRIGHT: Lünendonk GmbH, Bad Wörishofen 2004 – State: 19.05.2004 (no warranty for company information)

B. Cover letter

Model of the cover letter that accompanied the dispatch of the questionnaire:

Ludwigshafen
University of Applied Sciences
INSTITUTE FOR INTERNATIONAL
MANAGEMENT CONSULTING (www.i-imc.de)

Dipl. jur. (Univ.) **Boris-Rolf Dieter**
Zwehrenbuehlstraße 63
D-72070 Tuebingen
Tel. (h): +49-(0)7071 / 400 792
Tel. (o): +49-(0)7034 / 15-45 82
E-Mail: buergy@t-online.de

B. R. Dieter - Zwehrenbuehlstraße 63 - 72070 Tübingen

Title
Name
Company
Function
Street

40547 B-Town

Tuebingen, 14.10.2004

Survey for a MBA dissertation about the topic „IT-Contract Management"
Our telephone call on the 7th of October 2004

Dear Participant (name),

thank you very much for your readiness as an expert in the field of Contract Management to co-operate in this survey. Together with the complementary dissertation the topic „IT-Consulting Contract Management" will be the first time in Germany treated scientifically with this questionnaire.

The questions in the survey forms are formulated in such a manner that no internal information of your company must be disclosed and that no conflict of interests may occur due to my full time employment at the SerCon GmbH. The answers only require your expert assessment concerning the ideal formation of a Contract Management function.

To give you a first impression of the planned research work with the title:

„Implementation and Optimisation of a Contract Management Function in the German IT-Consulting Industry: An Exploration to which Extent a Company in the IT-Consulting Industry Can Benefit from a Contract Management Function"

72

I will provide you at your discretion with the dissertation proposal or the actual table of contents of the dissertation.

Supervising institution for this research work is the off-the-job MBA program of the **Institute for International Management Consulting of the University of Applied Sciences Ludwigshafen** (www.i-imc.de).

Participants of the survey will obtain, if desired, an exemplar of the appraisal. Please endorse this when re-dispatching the questionnaire forms.

Hoping the questions and the approximately 15 minutes that you will need to fill out the forms will be interesting I will be at your disposal for any queries.

Please send back the filled out questionnaire forms for evaluation if possible until the **22.10.2004**.

Looking forward to your answers I remain

with best regards

Boris-Rolf Dieter

Enclosure:
Questionnaire forms
University confirmation

Privacy Statement

All information provided will be strictly confidential. Especially the contact information will not be given away or published.

C. Questionnaire form

Model of the questionnaire that was used for the survey:

Ludwigshafen
University of Applied Sciences
INSTITUTE FOR INTERNATIONAL
MANAGEMENT CONSULTING
(www.i-imc.de)

Dipl. jur. (Univ.) **Boris-Rolf Dieter**
Zwehrenbuehlstraße 63
D-72070 Tuebingen
Tel.(h): +49-(0)7071 / 400 792
Tel. (o): +49-(0)7034 / 15-45 82
E-Mail: buergy@t-online.de

IT-Consulting Contract Management Survey

Thank you for your participation in this survey concerning (Sales) Contract Management (= CM) functions[106] in the German IT-Consulting industry[107]!

Your name:	
Your function:	
Your company / institution:	
Your e-mail address for queries:	
Your phone number for queries:	

---

[106] this means (Contract Management) functions that are dealing with sales contracts and additional activities and that support parts or the whole life cycle of such contracts

[107] the German IT-Consulting industry includes, according to the so-called „Luenendonk list", German companies that are creating their turnover predominantly with IT-Consulting, development of individual software or systems integration

Question 1 (strategic alignment):

Which ideal strategic alignment should have a CM function in the IT-Consulting industry?

a) focus:
primary focus on risk minimisation ☐
or
primary focus on maximisation of turnover ☐

and

b) customer contact:
predominantly direct customer contact (e.g. negotiation lead) ☐
or
predominantly indirect customer contact (e.g. sales back office) ☐

Annotations: ....

Question 2 (resource allocation):

Which allocation of CM resources would you consider in the IT-Consulting industry as ideal?

a) local allocation:
centralised (e.g. in the company´s headquarters) ☐
decentralised (e.g. in several locations) ☐
merged function ☐

and

b) thematic allocation:
according to geographical aspects (e.g. regions) ☐
according to topical aspects (e.g. products) ☐
multidimensional (e.g. according to projects and certain contracts) ☐
no thematic allocation ☐

Annotations: ....

Question 3 (hierarchical integration):

Which hierarchical integration do you consider as <u>ideal</u> for a CM function in the IT-Consulting industry?

a) organisational integration:
as administrative function (e.g. as a cost centre) ☐
as operative function (e.g. as a profit centre) ☐

and

b) hierarchical independence:
CM forms an own department ☐
CM is sub-division of an (other) department (e.g. Legal or project management) ☐
CM staff is incorporated in other departments ☐

Annotations: ....

Question 4 (reporting line):

Which reporting line do you consider as <u>ideal</u> for a CM function in the IT-Consulting industry?

to the manager of the Legal department ☐
to the CEO ☐
to the CFO ☐
to the manager of the or a business unit ☐
to the Operations manager ☐
to the CIO ☐
to others (please name examples): ....

Annotations: ....

Question 5 (tasks and disciplines):

Which phases of the CM process should a CM function in the IT-Consulting industry <u>in the ideal case</u> cover and which significance has this CM support for the company´s success?

a) phases:
1. presales ☐
2. bid / no-bid decision ☐
3. proposal design ☐
4. contract conclusion ☐
5. contract fulfilment ☐
6. contract closeout or termination and closure ☐

b) significance of the CM support for the company´s success:

1. for presales

1	2	3	4	5	6	7	8	9	10

low ... high

2. for the bid / no-bid decision

1	2	3	4	5	6	7	8	9	10

low ... high

3. for proposal design

1	2	3	4	5	6	7	8	9	10

low ... high

4. for contract conclusion

1	2	3	4	5	6	7	8	9	10

low ... high

5. for contract fulfilment

1	2	3	4	5	6	7	8	9	10

low ... high

6. for contract closeout etc.

1	2	3	4	5	6	7	8	9	10

low ... high

Annotations: ....

Question 6 (qualification and skills):

Which qualification and important skills form the <u>ideal</u> competence portfolio of a CM professional in the IT-Consulting industry?

a) qualification:

apprenticeship ☐

           field of apprenticeship:

                                  technical ☐
                                  commercial ☐
                                  others (please name) ....

or

study   ☐

           course of study: academy of applied sciences (BA) ☐
                             university of applied sciences (FH) ☐
                             university (Univ.) ☐

                 field of study: law (Univ.) ☐
                               economic law (FH) ☐
                               business administration ☐
                               business engineering ☐
                             others (please name) ....

b) skills:

technical understanding ☐
industry knowledge and experience ☐
project management skills ☐
negotiation know-how ☐
substantial communication and social competence ☐
language knowledge (e.g. legal English) ☐
experience as trainer ☐
(CM-) process understanding ☐
other skills (please name) ....

Annotations: ....

78

Question 7 (size of the CM function):

Which parameters can help to find the <u>ideal</u> size of a CM function in the IT-Consulting industry?

a) parameter:
turnover per (experienced) CM employee ☐
number of proposal writer etc. per (experienced) CM employee ☐
ratio of turnover to budget of the CM function ☐
number of contracts per (experienced) CM employee ☐
other parameters (please name): ....

b) ideal parameter expression:
ideal turnover per (experienced) CM employee ......Mio. EUR
ideal number of proposal writers etc. per (experienced) CM employee .. persons
ideal ratio of turnover to budget of the CM function % of turnover
ideal number of contracts per (experienced) CM employee ....contracts
other ideal parameter expressions (please name) ....

Annotations: ....

Question 8 (financial benefit):

Which <u>direct</u> financial benefit do you see in the activities of a CM function in the IT-Consulting industry?

Please name 3 specific examples (if possible with calculation logic):

1. ....
2. ....
3. ....

Question 9 (problem areas):

What do you consider as the <u>most important</u> problem areas for CM functions in the IT-Consulting industry?

Please name 5 specific problem areas:

1. ....
2. ....
3. ....
4. ....
5. ....

*****

Other general remarks or notes (at your discretion):

....
....
....
....

Thank you for your support and co-operation!

D. Appraisal of the Survey (in German)

Institute for International
Management Consulting
Ludwigshafen University
of Applied Sciences

„Auswertung der
IT-Consulting Contract Management Umfrage 2004"
Stand: 31.10.2004

Der Autor[108] dankt nochmals allen Teilnehmer der Umfrage für Ihre Unterstützung bei dieser in Deutschland erstmaligen Befragung von Experten im Vertragswesens bezüglich (vertriebsseitiger) Contract Management (= CM) Funktionen[109] in der deutschen IT-Consulting Branche[110].

Die Untersuchung ist Teil der MBA-Diplomarbeit des Autors (Titel: *„Implementation and Optimisation of a Contract Management Function in the German IT-Consulting Industry: An Exploration to which Extend a Company in the IT-Consulting Industry Can Benefit from a Contract Management Function"*; Veröffentlichung: Frühjahr 2005; dann erhältlich gegen eine Schutzgebühr beim Autor) im berufsbegleitenden Aufbaustudiumsprogramm des „Institutes for International Management Consulting" an der Hochschule für Wirtschaft FH Ludwigshafen/Rhein (www.i-imc.de).

Nachfolgend finden Sie die Auswertung der Ergebnisse für Ihren persönlichen Gebrauch. Eine Weitergabe an Dritte, auch in der eigenen Organisation, oder eine Veröffentlichung, auch in Auszügen, ist nur mit Zustimmung des Autors statthaft.

---

[108] Boris-Rolf Dieter, Dipl. jur. (Univ. Mannheim), MBA (Mai 2005), Zwehrenbühlstr. 63, 72070 Tübingen, 07071-400 792, buergy@t-online.de; Jahrgang 1969, verheiratet, ein Kind, war nach Studium (Mannheim und Toulon) und Rechtsreferendariat (Ravensburg, Speyer, Bonn und Windhoek) 6 Jahre im Vertragswesen einer IBM-Konzerngesellschaft tätig und wechselte dort 2004 in eine Personalreferentenposition

[109] damit sind hier (Vertragswesen-) Funktionen gemeint, die sich mit Vertriebsverträgen sowie dazugehörigen Aktivitäten befassen und Teile des oder den ganzen Lebenszyklus dieser Verträge begleiten

[110] die deutsche IT-Consulting Branche umfasst gemäß der sog. „Lünendonkliste" deutsche Unternehmen, deren Schwerpunkt der Geschäftstätigkeit das IT-Consulting, die Entwicklung von Individualsoftware und die Systemintegration bildet

Teilnehmerzahl:	23 (von 31 kontaktierten = ca. 74% Rücklauf)
davon CM-Praktiker der Zielbranche:	18
davon CM-nahe Akademiker oder Verbandsangehörige:	5
Anzahl teilnehmender IT-Consulting Firmen der Lünendonkliste:	18 von 25 (72%) -> jeweils pro Unternehmen ein Experte aus dem Bereich „Contract Management"
Erhebungsgebiet:	Deutschland; IT-Consulting Branche
Erhebungszeitraum:	Oktober 2004

Ergebnisse der Umfrage[111]:

Frage 1 (strategische Ausrichtung):

Welche strategische Ausrichtung sollte eine CM-Funktion in der IT-Consulting Branche idealerweise haben?

a) Fokus:
primäre Ausrichtung auf Risikominimierung   **81%**
primäre Ausrichtung auf Umsatzmaximierung   **19%**

Anmerkungen: Einige Teilnehmer sehen beide Ziele als gleichrangig an. Als Ziel wird in diesem Zusammenhang „Gewinnmaximierung" als Kombination der beiden o.g. Ziele genannt.

b) Kundenkontakt:
vorwiegend direkter Kundenkontakt (z.B. als Verhandlungsführer)   **60%**
vorwiegend indirekter Kundenkontakt (z.B. als „Backoffice" des Vertriebs)   **40%**

Anmerkungen: Es wurde von Teilnehmern darauf hingewiesen, dass insbesondere bei größeren Verträgen ein direkter Kundenkontakt sinnvoll ist. Bei kleineren Verträgen ist eine Rücksprache des Vertriebs bei der CM-Funktion bei der Über- oder Unterschreitung bestimmter Vertragsparameter ausreichend. Hier können dann auch taktische Aspekte eine Rolle spielen wann und wann nicht CM indirekt oder direkt Kundenkontakt hat (z.B. „bad guy" / „good guy" Spiel), aber auch der Reifegrad der CM-Funktion selbst oder von deren (internen) Kunden. Vorgeschlagen wird auch eine Zweiteilung der Funktion (vor Ort umsatzgesteuert mit direktem Kundenkontakt und im Backoffice risikominimierend mit eher indirektem Kundenkontakt).

---

[111] die Prozentwerte wurden auf Vorkommastellen gerundet, es können sich dadurch unerhebliche Differenzen der Summenwerte ergeben (z.B. Summe ergibt nicht 100%)

Frage 2 (Ressourcenallokation):

Welche Zuordnung der CM-Ressourcen sehen Sie in der IT-Consulting Branche als ideal an?

a) lokale Zuordnung:

zentral (z.b. Sitz in der Unternehmenszentrale)	30%
dezentral (z.b. Sitz in den Niederlassungen)	17%
Mischform	52%

b) thematische Zuordnung:

nach geographischen Aspekten (z.b. Regionen)	17%
nach themenspezifischen Aspekten (z.b. Produkte)	26%
nach mehreren Aspekten (z.b. Projekte und Vertragsarten)	48%
keine thematische Zuordnung	9%

Anmerkungen: Es wurde von Teilnehmern genannt, dass eine thematische Zuordnung auch nach Sprachen/Sprachregionen, Key Accounts oder Branchen sinnvoll vorgenommen werden könnte. Sie sollte in jedem Fall an die Organisation des Vertriebsbereich und/oder dem Produkt/Leistungsportfolio des Unternehmens angelehnt sein.

Frage 3 (hierarchische Integration):

Welche hierarchische Integration sollte bei einer CM-Funktion in der IT-Consulting Branche idealerweise umgesetzt sein?

a) organisatorische Einordnung:

als Stabsfunktion (z.B. cost centre)	78%
als operative Funktion (z.B. profit centre)	22%

b) hierarchische Unabhängigkeit:

CM ist eigene Abteilung	39%
CM ist Teil einer (anderen) Abteilung (z.B. Recht oder Projektmanagement)	48%
CM-Mitarbeiter sind in verschiedene Abteilungen integriert	13%

Anmerkungen: Es wurde von einigen Teilnehmern darauf hingewiesen, dass unabhängig von der hierarchischen Integration einer CM-Funktion immer eine gewisse operative Unabhängigkeit (gegenüber dem Vertrieb etc.) zugestanden werden muss. Allerdings sollte auch eine möglichst große Nähe zur Vertriebs- oder Projektorganisation angestrebt werden, um Berührungsängste zu minimieren, das Verständnis der jeweiligen Rahmenbedingungen zu vertiefen und den Informationsfluss zu optimieren. Vorgeschlagen wurde neben den o.g. Abteilungen auch eine Einordnung von CM in das Controlling, den Einkauf, das Projektteam oder die Qualitätssicherung.

Frage 4 (Berichtweg):

Welchen Berichtsweg halten Sie für eine CM-Funktion in der IT-Consulting Branche am <u>sinnvollsten</u>?

An den Leiter Rechtsabteilung	16%
An den CEO (Geschäftsführer, Vorstand etc.)	45%
An den Leiter Finanz o.ä.	3%
An einen Leiter Geschäftsbereich o.ä.	29%
An den Leiter Verwaltung	3%
An den CIO o.ä. (Leiter IT etc.)	3%

Anmerkungen: Weitere Varianten für einen Berichtsweg wurden von den Teilnehmern nicht genannt.

Frage 5 (Aufgaben und Tätigkeiten):

Welche Phasen des CM-Prozesses sollte eine CM-Funktion in der IT-Consulting Branche <u>idealerweise</u> abdecken und welche Bedeutung hat die CM-Unterstützung für den Unternehmenserfolg?

a) Phasen:

1. Akquiseunterstützung („presales")	39%
2. Angebotsentscheidung („bid / no-bid decision")	52%
3. Angebotserstellung („proposal design")	74%
4. Vertragsschluss („contract conclusion")	74%
5. Vertragserfüllung („contract fulfilment")	61%
6. Vertragsbeendigung („contract closeout or termination and closure")	78%

b) Bedeutung der CM-Unterstützung für den Unternehmenserfolg (1 = niedrig; 10 = hoch):

1. bei der Akquiseunterstützung	Durchschnittswert: 3,4
2. bei der Angebotsentscheidung	Durchschnittswert: 4,8
3. bei der Angebotserstellung	Durchschnittswert: 7,4
4. beim Vertragsschluss	Durchschnittswert: 7,3
5. bei der Vertragserfüllung	Durchschnittswert: 5,0
6. bei der Vertragsbeendigung	Durchschnittswert: 5,9

Frage 6 (Qualifikation und Kompetenzen):

Welche Qualifikation und wichtige Kompetenzen sollte ein CM-Mitarbeiter in der IT-Consulting Branche idealerweise haben?

a) Qualifikation:

Alle Teilnehmer sehen für eine CM-Tätigkeit ein Studium als erforderliche Qualifikation an.

präferierte Studienart:	Berufsakademie (BA)	18%
	Fachhochschule (FH)	38%
	Universität (Univ.)	38%

präferierte Studienrichtung:	Recht (Univ.)	29%
	Wirtschaftsrecht (FH)	29%
	BWL	24%
	Wirtschaftsingenieurwesen	18%

Zusätzlich wurden Informatik, Wirtschaftsinformatik und Ingenieurwesen als relevante Studienrichtungen und auch Doppelqualifikationen (wie Jura plus MBA) genannt.

Für eine Lehre sprachen sich 19% der Teilnehmer aus. Dabei wurde überwiegend eine kaufmännische Lehre empfohlen, teils aber auch eine technische Lehre oder eine Lehre mit Schwerpunkt auf Qualitätsmanagent und –sicherung. Allerdings wurde eine Lehre nur als Zusatzqualifikation zu einem Studium gesehen, nicht aber als alleinige Qualifikation für eine CM-Tätigkeit.

b) Kompetenzen:

Technisches Verständnis	78%
Branchenkenntnis oder –erfahrung	83%
Projektmanagementkenntnisse	70%
Vertragsverhandlungsknow-how	83%
fundierte Kommunikations- / Sozialkompetenz	87%
Sprachkenntnisse (z.B. legal English)	57%
Erfahrung als Schulungsreferent	9%
(CM-) Prozessverständnis	83%

Zusätzlich wurden genannt: Stressresistenz, Reisewilligkeit, juristische Kompetenz (Vertragsrecht), Kenntnisse in Qualitätsmanagement und -sicherung, Know-how bezüglich Risikoabschätzung, Risikomanagementerfahrungen, IT-fachliche Kenntnisse, Erfahrungen mit Angeboten und Verträgen sowie mit Problemfällen der Vertragspraxis in der Branche.

Frage 7 (Größe der CM-Funktion):

Mit welchen Parametern kann man die <u>ideale</u> Größe einer CM-Funktion in der IT-Consulting Branche überschlägig bemessen?

a) Parameter:

Umsatzhöhe pro (erfahrenem) CM-Mitarbeiter	**9%**
Anzahl Angebotsersteller o.ä. pro (erfahrenem) CM-Mitarbeiter	**26%**
Verhältnis Umsatzhöhe zu Budget der CM-Funktion	**0%**
Anzahl der Verträge pro (erfahrenem) CM-Mitarbeitern	**65%**

Als weitere Parameter wurden genannt: Anzahl der zu modifizierenden Standardverträge, Anzahl der Kundentermine, Anzahl der Eskalationen im Projektverlauf oder Anzahl extern (Kunden, Lieferanten) vorgegebener Verträge.

b) ideale Parameterausprägungen:

Hier gab es nur wenige Nennungen, die teils sehr weit voneinander abweichen (Umsatzhöhe: 10-20 Mio. EUR bzw. 100 Mio. EUR; Angebotsersteller: 10, 12-15 bzw. 120; Umsatzhöhe: keine Angaben; Verträge: 15 pro Woche, 20-30, 50 bzw. 160 p.a.), da die Parameterausprägungen nach Ansicht vieler Teilnehmer zu stark von den individuellen Rahmenbedingungen des Unternehmens abhängen.

Als Rahmenbedingungen wurden genannt: Standardisierungsgrad, Vertragsumfang, Vertragsart, Vertriebs/Geschäftsmodell, Erfahrung des Vertriebs in Vertragsfragen, Grad der Vorarbeiten der Angebotsersteller, Komplexität der Verträge, Problemgrad der Kundenbeziehung, Leistungsumfang, Art und Umfang der Projekte oder vom Auftraggeber vorgegebene technische, kommerzielle und rechtliche Bedingungen.

Frage 8 (finanzieller Nutzen):

Welchen <u>direkten</u> finanziellen Nutzen sehen Sie in der Arbeit einer CM-Funktion in der IT-Consulting Branche?

Von den Teilnehmern hierfür genannte Beispiele in der Zusammenfassung:

1. Erhöhung der Erfolgsquote von Angeboten
2. präventive Vermeidung typischer Risiken und Fehler bei Vertragsgestaltung (insbesondere bei Werkverträgen), Kalkulation (insbesondere bei Festpreisen), Leistungsbeschreibung, Leistungsabgrenzung, Mitwirkungspflichten und Projektplanung (Profitsicherung durch Risikominimierung)
3. Sicherung des Honoraranspruchs durch professionelle Anspruchswahrung und - durchsetzung
4. Vermeidung unnötiger Haftungsrisiken durch sinnvolle Haftungsregelungen und Vermeidung typischer Haftungsfälle

5. Durchsetzung oder Vereinbarung niedriger Gewährleistungsfristen statt der gesetzlichen 24 Monate (reduziert Gewährleistungsaufwände- und –zeiträume sowie den Rückstellungsbedarf)
6. Begrenzung von Schadenssummen in Streitfällen
7. konsistentes und bewußtes Eingehen bzw. Vermeiden von Risiken
8. direkte Beeinflussung der Kundenzufriedenheit (relevant für Folge- und Zusatzgeschäft) und der Unternehmensreputation durch Vertrags- und Projektmanagement „at cost", „in time" und „at quality"
9. Kostensenkungseffekte aufgrund effektiven Risikomanagements
10. Erkennung von Verbesserungspotential
11. Vermeidung von Vertragsstrafen und pauschalierten Schadensersatzregelungen oder zumindest summarische Begrenzung in Verträgen
12. Minimierung des Aufwandes in der Akquistionsphase durch Erstellung von Templates (auch kundenspezifische)
13. Durchsetzung von Standards gegenüber Kunden
14. einheitliche (CM-) Prozesse
15. konsistente Vertragsinhalte
16. rechtliche Qualifizierung (Leistungsabgrenzung) neuer Anforderungen durch den Kunden als Gewährleistungsfall (kostenfrei) oder Change Request (kostenpflichtig), dadurch Generierung von Folge- und Neuaufträgen und Minimierung von ungeplanten Mehraufwänden
17. Verhinderung der (für Auftragnehmer sehr unvorteilhaften) Rückabwicklung gefährdeter Projekte durch Verhandlungen
18. Verhandlung günstiger Konditionen
19. Einsparung von Gebühren externer Rechtsberater
20. Durchführung und Kontrolle komplexer Vergütungsmechanismen
21. zielführende, auftragnehmerfreundliche und praktikable (sowie rechtssichere) Gestaltung von Vertragsklauseln (z.B. Abnahme, Haftung, Sicherheiten, Versicherungen etc.)
22. durch regelmäßiges Reviews im Rahmen der Delivery Phase erhebliche Reduktion des Risikos des Scheiterns eines Projektes und der Anzahl der Problemprojekte
23. Standardisierung von Vertragsarten / Vertragsklauseln / Vertragswerken zur Risikominimierung, Beschleunigung der Durchlaufzeiten und Erhöhung der Vertragsqualität

Frage 9 (Problembereiche):

Was sehen Sie als derzeit <u>wichtigste</u> Problembereiche für CM-Funktionen in der IT-Consulting Branche?

Von den Teilnehmern hierfür genannte Problembereiche in der Zusammenfassung:

1. Projekte und Verträge technisch, rechtlich und wirtschaftlich durchschaubar machen, um sie kalkulierbar zu machen
2. Arbeiten mit den komplexen Entscheidungsstrukturen des Unternehmens

3. Balancing von Risiko und Aufwand, etwa Vereinbarung von Businessanforderungen und gesetzlichen Anforderungen (z.b. erhöhter Verwaltungsaufwand durch Sarbanes-Oxley-Act, Bilanzierungsvorgaben nach US-GAAP)
4. Vertragsmanagement als direkter CRM-Einflussfaktor
5. unzulängliche Zeit- und Ressourcenplanung, Ergebnisorientierung (Beschreibung von Arbeitspaketen), Beistellungsmanagement des Kunden, Phasenkalkulation und rechtliche Absicherung
6. Spannungsverhältnis zwischen Vertrieb und CM (Kosten-Nutzen-Frage: generelle Kostenproblematik von Stabsstellen, Positionierung von CM nicht als Admin-Aufgabe, sondern als value add)
7. nicht erfolgte oder verspätete (dann auch oft fehlendes Hintergrundwissen) Involvierung von CM bei Angeboten
8. Nichteinbeziehung von CM bzw. Übergehen des negativen CM-Votums bei Vertragsabschlüssen (unklare Verantwortlichkeit, Rollenverständnis und Entscheidungskompetenzen)
9. Vertragsstrafen, Erfolgsgarantien und „Risk-Sharing"
10. Weisungsgebundenheit bei Eingliederung in den operative Bereich
11. zu ausgeprägte Kundensicht bei längerem Engagement
12. Durchlaufgeschwindigkeit von Angebots- und Vertragsabwicklung
13. erhöhte Anforderungen im Rahmen öffentlicher und privater Ausschreibungen (erhöhter Verwaltungsaufwand)
14. zunehmende Komplexität von Verträgen und wachsende Unklarheit bezüglich Aufgabenstellungen
15. Kompetenzen und Fähigkeiten (z.B. Mangel an übergreifendem fachlichen Know-how)
16. Vergütungssystematik (z.B. Bonus-Malus-Regelungen bei der Vergütung)
17. Rechtsunsicherheit wegen fehlender Rechtsprechung
18. abschließende Leistungsdefinition und –abgrenzung zur Haftungsreduzierung
19. Versicherbarkeit von Haftungsrisiken
20. unterschiedliche Ansatzpunkte von operativem Bereich und CM im Bezug auf die Relevanz von vertraglichen Punkten
21. Abgrenzung zu Rechtsabteilungen
22. Existenzfrage (CM wird nicht als notwendig erachtet)
23. Transparenzfrage (CM-Funktion vermittelt oft nicht erfolgreich was für Aufgaben sie wahrnimmt)
24. Schwierigkeit das oft sehr breite Angebotsspektrum mit standardisierten Diensten zu beschreiben und damit entsprechende wiederkehrende Muster über ein Standardangebot hinaus zu unterstützen
25. Risikoabwälzung der Kunden auf den Dienstleister durch einseitige Vertragsbedingungen (insbesondere im Bereich der Großkunden)
26. durch immer stärkere Internationalisierung des Business, besteht die Notwendigkeit mit nicht unerheblichen Aufwand Kenntnisse mehrerer Rechtsräume und deren Gepflogenheiten aufzubauen
27. CM hat als Schnittstellenfunktion extrem hohen (internen) Abstimmungs- und Kommunikationsbedarf (Projektmanagement, Vertrieb, Delivery Units), das selbe gilt extern für komplexe Verträge
28. Soft Skills (Teamarbeit)

*****

Der Autor wünscht nun viel Erfolg bei der Nutzung und Einbeziehung der Ergebnisse in Ihre CM-Tätigkeit und steht für Rückfragen gerne zur Verfügung!

XV. ....Instead of an Epilogue

After all the above mentioned facts and figures about how to optimise or implement a CM function two simple aspects should be kept in mind:

"Management that wants to change an institution must first show it loves that institution."

John Tusa [112]

"My love for any place, or person, or institution is exactly the measure of my desire to reform them."

Thomas Arnold [113]

The author hopes that the information and incitements delivered with this compilation are helpful and inspiring for the reader and perhaps a starting point for further research in this special topic of legal and business administration.

For the author working in this area the first years of his professional life was a fine preparation for a general business career and as a graduate lawyer an exciting experience about the interfaces between law and business administration.

---

[112] British broadcaster and radio journalist (*1936), "Observer", 27th February 1994, in "Sayings of the week"
[113] British historian and educator (*1795, +1842), in David Newsome "Godliness and Good Learning" (1961)

XVI. Bibliography

Not all of the listed literature was used for references but in all cases for general reading about the publication topic. While a bibliography for this topic does not yet exist, all literature found during the research concerning the publication topic even in a wider sense is presented below. Referenced literature is additionally marked with an asterisk (*).

Aberdeen Group*
Contract Optimization: A Recession-Proof Strategy for Maximizing Performance and Minimizing Risks (2003), an executive white paper by Aberdeen Group , Inc. (www.aberdeen.com), Boston

Aberdeen Group*
The Sales Contract Management Competitive Framework (2004), article with Contract Management design models for different levels of competitive frameworks (laggards, below norm, industry norm, above norm, best in class); www.aberdeen.com/cm%2Dcoe/default.asp

Bartsch, M.*
Qualitätssicherung für Softwareprojekte durch Vertragsgestaltung und Vertragsmanagement (Quality Assurance for Software Projects through Contract Design and Contract Management), Springer, in "Informatik-Spektrum" January 2000, p. 3 ff

Bausinger, S.*
Implementierung eines Vertragsmanagement bei der ESCAD Engineering GmbH (Implementation of a Contract Management at the ESCAD Engineering Ltd.) (2002), dissertation at the University of Applied Sciences, Pforzheim

Bruhn, M.
Qualitätsmanagement für Dienstleistungen: Grundlagen, Konzepte, Methoden (Quality Management for Services: Basics, Concepts, Methods) (2003), 4th improved edition, Springer, Berlin

Bühner, R.*
Betriebswirtschaftliche Organisationslehre (Theory of Commercial Organisation) (1999), 9th edition, Oldenbourg, Munich/Vienna

Garrett, G. A.*
World Class Contracting (1997), ESI International, Arlington

Heussen, B.*
Vertragsmanagement und Vertragsgestaltung (Contract Management and Contract Design) (1997), Otto Schmidt, Cologne

Heussen, B.*
Rechtliches Risikomanagement (Legal Risk Management) (2002), script for the EUROFORUM conference "Unternehmensjuristentage 2002 (company laywers´ days 2002)", 26th and 27th February 2002 in Frankfurt/Main

Höfner, C.
Contract Management – added value für IT-Outsourcing- und Serviceprojekte (Contract Management – Added Value for IT-Outsourcing and Service Projects) (2004), presentation for the DGRI study group for company lawyers on the 23rd of January in Frankfurt/Main at the DekaBank Deutsche Girozentrale

IACCM*
Contracting as a Strategic Competence (2003), article about contracting as a source of competitive advantages; www.iaccm.com/libary

IACCM*
Contract Management – An Opportunity Still Being Missed? (2003), article about the IACCM Contract Management study; www.iaccm.com/library

IACCM*
IACCM Corporate Benchmarking Survey (2004), world-wide and cross-industry survey about Contract Management activities (cited for Sales Contract Management); www.iaccm.com/benchmarking/research/intro.php

IACCM*
Contract Management learning units:
Chapter 1 "How Contractual Relationships Are Formed & Why They Matter" (2004),
Chapter 2 "Getting to a Winning Position" (2004),
Chapter 3 "Overview of Major Types of Relationship" (2004);
www.iaccm.org/libary

IACCM*
IACCM Master Agreement Survey (2004), world-wide and cross-industry survey about master agreement usage and policies (cited for Sales Contracts), www.iaccm.com/survey/masteragreement/results/index.php?rolesel=2

IACCM*
The Commercial Function: Evolution and Background (2003), article about the development and history of Contract Management functions, www.iaccm.org/library

Kapellmann, K. D. (editor)*
Juristisches Projektmanagement bei Entwicklung und Realisierung von Bauprojekten (Legal Project Management in the Development and Realisation of Construction Projects), (1997), Werner, Düsseldorf

Krappé, K., Kallayil, G.*
Contract Management Is More out of Control Than You Think (2003), survey about Contract Management maturity, in "Journal of Contract Management", April 2003 edition, National Contract Management Association (NCMA), McLean (Virginia)

Kubr, M. (editor)*
Management Consulting: A Guide to the Profession (1996), 3rd edition, International Labour Office, Geneva

Kulartz, H.-P.*
IT-Leistungen: fehlerfreie Ausschreibungen und rechtssichere Vertragsinhalte (IT-Services: Accurate Public Invitation to Tender and Legally Secured Contract Contents) (2002), Bundesanzeiger, Cologne

Lichtenberg, G.
Risikomanagement bei EDV-Projekten (Risk Management in IT-Projects) (1992), Expert, Ehningen

Maister, D. H.*
Managing the Professional Service Firm (2003, paperback edition), Simon & Schuster UK, London

Nextance Advisory Services*
Enhance your Business Performance by Adopting Best Practices in Contract Management (2004), white paper about best practices in Contract Management; www.nextance.com

Niedereichholz, C.
Qualitätsmanagement in der Unternehmensberatung (Quality Management in the Consulting Practise) (1996), Recht und Praxis, Kissing

Niedereichholz, C. I*
Unternehmensberatung Bd. I – Beratungsmarketing und Auftragsakquisition (Management Consulting Vol. I – Consulting Marketing and Project Acquisition) (2001), 3rd edition, Oldenbourg, Munich/Vienna

Niedereichholz, C. II*
Unternehmensberatung Bd. II – Auftragsdurchführung und Qualitätssicherung (Management Consulting Vol. II – Project Realisation and Quality Assurance) (2003), 3rd edition, Oldenbourg, Munich/Vienna

Porter, M. E.*
Competitive Advantage: Creating and Sustaining Superior Performance (1985), The Free Press, New York

PricewaterhouseCoopers LLP*
Contract management: control value and minimise risks (2003), independent paper by PricewaterhouseCoopers LLP (www.pwc.com) sponsored by Memba Limited (www.memba.com), London

Quiring, A.
Die rechtliche Absicherung der Unternehmensberatung (The Legal Safeguarding of a Consulting Practise) (1996), Recht und Praxis, Kissing

Treuhandanstalt
Dokumentation 1990-1994: Band 7 (Documentation 1990-1994: Volume 7) (1994) "Vertragsmanagement" p. 833-1033, Treuhandanstalt Direktorat Kommunikation/Medien

Tybussek, B.*
Praktisches Vertragsrecht und Vertragsmanagement – Fallstudien für Wirtschaftsjuristen im 4. Semester (Practical Contract Law and Contract Management – Case Studies for 4th term business law students), (2002), University of Applied Sciences, Pforzheim

Ury, W.*
Getting Past No (1993), Bantam Books, New York

Wöhe, G.*
Einführung in die Allgemeine Betriebswirtschaftslehre (Introduction to the General Industrial Management Theory) (2002), 21st edition, Vahlen, Munich

XVII. Acknowledgements

First of all the author thanks his wife Michaela Forster-Dieter. From his first thoughts about such a postgraduate study she supported these plans and assisted him during the occasionally very challenging two and a half years of the MBA-program with her own experience in two postgraduate study programs, a lot of love, patience and much understanding. And this even when this meant that she had to spend a lot of time on her own while the leisure time and nights of the author were often dedicated to the MBA-course. The author hopes that he can render all this in the next joint "night and day project" that started in November with the birth of their first child.

The author also thanks his lecturer and supervisor Karl Adolf Scholz for his inspirations and the workload he invested in the support of the dissertation proposal and the dissertation itself. Through sharing his vast management experience in the consulting industry with the author, he had a major influence in the direction, quality and progress of the dissertation.

A special thanks goes to his friend and professional companion Gregor Schulz for his constant and dedicated help through the dissertation process and his motivating interest in the dissertation topic. Starting from first sketches of the work years ago for a planned article in a magazine up to the dissertation proposal and the dissertation itself he was always personally committed and deeply interested to support this project.

The author owes his parents as well a special thanks because they supported the work through accommodating the author in his home town Mannheim during his course days in Ludwigshafen.

The author thanks all Contract Management professionals who have contributed to the data collection and especially his fellow MBA students Birgit Seiferth and Peter Link for many useful hints and information. The review of the survey forms and the survey appraisal was supported by Stefan Dittrich; the editorial reading was done by Emma Condon and Gregor Schulz.

The author also thanks the following academics for their help in collecting and validating the necessary data and for their hints for sources of knowledge about the dissertation topic (in alphabetic order): Prof. Dr. Klaus Detzer (University of Applied Sciences Reutlingen), RA Prof. Dr.

Andreas Quiring (University of Applied Sciences Ludwigshafen/Rhine) and Prof. Dr. Annette Tybussek (University of Applied Sciences Pforzheim).

An additional thank is directed to the following professional associations that helped in getting in contact with important subject matter experts, in unclosing significant sources of data and in adding an objective views on this industry topic: IACCM namely Holger Ehnes (Focal Point Germany), Robert Peak (Advisory Board Member), Simon Roberts (Director Member Services) and Tim Cummins (Executive Director) and BITKOM namely Dr. Matthias Weber (Head of Department IT Services and Knowledge Management).

For her time sponsorship and infrastructural support of the dissertation a particular thanks is owed to the author´s employer, the SerCon GmbH, a German IBM Business Consulting Services affiliate, and particularly his former superior Mr. Daniel Wallner, head of the Risk & Contract Management department and the Quality Management function, and his actual superior Mrs. Beate Riepe, head of the Human Resources department.

XVIII. About the Author

The author, Boris-Rolf Dieter, born on the 5th of July 1969 in Mannheim (Germany), studied Law at the University of Mannheim and a year abroad at the University of Toulon (France). After his graduation in Law he attended as junior lawyer the legal apprenticeship program of the ministry of justice of the German federal Land Baden-Wuerttemberg with stages in Ravensburg, Speyer, Windhoek (Namibia) and Bonn.

In 1998 he started his professional career in the Contract Management department of the SerCon GmbH, a German IT-Consulting affiliate of IBM Business Consulting Services. There he was appointed in 2001 as Senior Expert. In 2004 he joined as Senior Assistant the HR department and was send 2005 on internal assignment to the IBM Germany headquarter as HR Recruitment Specialist.

Since 2000 he lives with his family in Tuebingen. His contact details for questions concerning the publication and cooperation inquiries are:

Boris-Rolf Dieter
Dipl. jur. (Univ.), MBA
Zwehrenbuehlstr. 63
D-72070 Tuebingen
+49-(0)7071-400 792
buergy@t-online.de